T0301293

The Role of Financial Markets in Achieving the Sustainable Development Goals

PROGRESSING THE SUSTAINABLE DEVELOPMENT GOALS SERIES

This timely series offers a multidisciplinary forum for the latest research on critical topics and issues related to the UN's Sustainable Development Goals. Focusing on these global targets and efforts to advance them, books in the series address some of the grand challenges facing society today.

For a full list of Edward Elgar published titles, including the titles in this series, visit our website at www.e-elgar.com.

The Role of Financial Markets in Achieving the Sustainable Development Goals

Edited by

Magdalena Ziolo

Full Professor of Finance, Faculty of Economics, Finance and Management, University of Szczecin, Poland

PROGRESSING THE SUSTAINABLE DEVELOPMENT GOALS SERIES

Cheltenham, UK · Northampton, MA, USA

Published by
Edward Elgar Publishing Limited
The Lypiatts
15 Lansdown Road
Cheltenham
Glos GL50 2JA
UK

Edward Elgar Publishing, Inc.
William Pratt House
9 Dewey Court
Northampton
Massachusetts 01060
USA

A catalogue record for this book
is available from the British Library

Library of Congress Control Number: 2024934594

This book is available electronically in the **Elgar**online
Economics subject collection
http://dx.doi.org/10.4337/9781035323265

ISBN 978 1 0353 2325 8 (cased)
ISBN 978 1 0353 2326 5 (eBook)

Printed and bound by CPI Group (UK) Ltd, Croydon, CR0 4YY

Contents

Figures

Tables

Contributors

EDITOR

Magdalena Ziolo is Professor at the University of Szczecin, Poland. Her research and teaching scope focus on finance, banking and sustainability. She has extensive experience gained in financial institutions. She has received scholarships from the Dekaban-Liddle Foundation (University of Glasgow, Scotland) and Impakt Asia Erasmus + (Ulan Bator, Mongolia). She is a Member of Polish Accreditation Commission, Member of the Financial Sciences Committee of PAS (the Polish Academy of Sciences), Member of the Advisory Scientific Committee of the Financial Ombudsman, Expert of the National Centre for Research and Development, Expert of the National Science Centre and the National Agency for Academic Exchange, and Expert of the Accreditation Agency of Curacao. She was a member of the State Quality Council, Kosovo Accreditation Agency and visiting professor at the University of Prishtina (Kosovo). She is Principal Investigator in the research projects funded by the National Science Center, Poland in the field of sustainable finance. She is the author and editor of numerous books, mostly about financing sustainable development.

CONTRIBUTORS

Iwona Bąk is an Associate Professor, PhD at West Pomeranian University of Technology Szczecin, Poland. She is an expert in the field of quantitative methods, specializing in analyses regarding the use of quantitative methods in economic research, with particular emphasis on international comparisons in the area of sustainable development, competitiveness of the national economy and regional development, and experience in working with advanced statistical packages: STATISTICA, R program, etc. She is the author and co-author of scientific articles published in scientific journals from the JCR list, and has practical experience in the implementation of projects carried out on behalf of public institutions.

Beata Zofia Filipiak is Professor at the University of Szczecin, Poland. She is the Head of the Department of Sustainable Finance and Capital Markets at the University of Szczecin, as well as a Member of the University Council of the University of Szczecin. Her research and teaching scope focus on finance, finance management in public sector and sustainability. She has extensive experience gained in financial institutions and financial markets. A scholarship holder of the Flemish government the University of Antwerp in 1999, she has also received scholarships from DAAD (2007–2008 and 2008–2009) and DPWS (2016–2018), Erasmus +. She is a Member of the Financial Sciences Committee of PAS (the Polish Academy of Sciences) and an Expert of The National Center for Research and Development (NCBR). She was an Expert of the Polish Accreditation Commission and a board member of the Polish Association of Finance and Banking. She has been a licensed financial advisor since 1998. She was involved in 26 scientific projects regarding: corporate financial strategies, financial strategies of LGU's and sustainable development. She carries out research supported by the National Science Center Poland in the scope of financing sustainable development. She is the author and editor of numerous books, mostly about financial management and financing sustainable development.

Research interests: sustainable finances; use of financial instruments ("green financial instruments") in creating sustainable development; ESG risk; financial strategies and their connection with business models; policy of public authorities towards sustainable development (instruments, decisions, effects).

Ewa Kulińska-Sadłocha has a PhD in economics and finance. Her research and teaching scope focus on cost accounting, banking and sustainability. She has over 20 years of teaching and organizational experience as a lecturer, as well as extensive experience gained in business practice: banking, accounting and controlling. She has received scholarships from the Osteuropa-Sonderprogramm (University of Zurich). She is the author and co-author of numerous scientific and popular scientific publications in the field of finance, controlling, sustainable development and social market economy. She is a member of the Polish Economic Society, Poznan Society of Friends of Sciences and the Editorial Committee of the scientific journal *Bezpieczny Bank/Safe Bank*.

Anna Spoz is Assistant Professor, PhD at the Department of Finance and Accountancy at the John Paul II Catholic University of Lublin, Poland. Her research and teaching scope focus on finance, particularly corporate finance, accounting and tax and sustainable finance. She is the author and co-author of numerous publications on finance, accounting, reporting, and management. She is a reviewer of international publications. She combines teaching and scholarly activities with work in the business.

Acknowledgment

We would like to thank the reviewer professor Zbysław Dobrowolski (Jagiellonian University, Poland) for his thoughtful comments and efforts towards improving our monograph.

1. Introduction to *The Role of Financial Markets in Achieving the Sustainable Development Goals*

Magdalena Ziolo

Contemporary financial markets are influenced by several financial and non-financial factors that determine the need to implement changes in banking and financial institutions. The dynamically changing environment creates new challenges for financial institutions and dilemmas for which existing solutions and mechanisms are insufficient. Progressing demographic, climatic, and socio-economic changes have their financial dimension and create a new type of risk – ESG (Environmental, Social, Governance) risk, which is currently one of the leading risk typologies. The most significant threat is caused by environmental risk and the associated reputational risk. These risks are substantial from the perspective of the assessment and functioning of banking and financial institutions. Climate change, social and financial exclusion, income inequality, loss of trust, and financialization are just some of the problems that contemporary financial markets must face. The issues of economic imbalance and financial instability also appear to be a significant challenge for modern finance and banking. Each of the phenomena mentioned above has specific consequences for finance and determines the change of business models of banking and financial institutions and the approach to their security and stability. Regulatory and supervisory institutions responsible for the quality of the regulatory and legal framework for financial markets in new socio-economic conditions face similar challenges and dilemmas. Counteracting undesirable climate, demographic, and socio-economic changes is achieved by implementing the postulates of sustainable development favoring social inclusion. An attempt to increase the alignment of finance and banking with the expectations of sustainable growth and development is their "greening" and catching the "blue wave." More broadly, sustainability is perceived as ensuring the equivalence of decision-making criteria (economic, social, and environmental) in decision-making processes in finance and banking. Green, responsible, sustainable, and blue finance and banking are some of the most dynamically developing subdisciplines of finance supporting sustainable growth and development processes.

Due to the increasing impact of ESG risk on economies and societies on a global scale, there is an urgent need to take remedial actions and mitigate the impact of this risk. ESG risk, including climate change risk, is currently one of the types of risks with the most significant importance and influence. ESG risk affects not only the operational activities of business entities, including their financial performance, but also the quality of life and public safety. Hence, all governments, states, and institutions worldwide are interested in this type of risk. Reducing ESG risk requires taking several actions to eliminate or reduce the sources of this risk, which are usually inherent in companies' business models based on unfriendly solutions that negatively impact the environment and society but also result from managerial and unethical activities. The negative environmental impact is visible in the so-called blue economy and unsustainable activities in other economic sectors. Taking remedial actions requires a long-term economic transformation plan and strategic tools (strategies, different business models). A type of such a plan is the Sustainable Development Goals (SDGs), which specify targets to be implemented under each of the 17 SDGs. There are 17 SDGs (SDG1 – No poverty; SDG2 – Zero hunger; SDG3 – Ensure healthy lives and promote well-being; SDG4 – Quality education; SDG5 – Gender equality; SDG6 – Clean water and sanitation; SDG7 – Affordable and clean energy; SDG8 – Decent work and economic growth; SDG9 – Industry innovation and infrastructure; SDG10 – Reduced inequalities; SDG11 – Sustainable cities and communities; SDG12 – Responsible consumption and production; SDG13 – Climate action; SDG14 – Life below water; SDG15 – Life on land; SDG16 – Peace, justice and strong institutions; SDG17 – Partnership for the goals) and 169 subordinated targets constituting a comprehensive action plan to ensure sustainable development. The SDGs refer to issues such as climate change, greening, and energy transformation, solving social problems such as hunger, poverty, exclusion, unequal treatment, and the so-called common issues, e.g., partnership for the SDGs or sustainable economic growth. The Sustainable Development Goals are aimed at reducing negative externalities related to human activities through issues of social inclusion (SDGs 1–11, 15,

16), environmental protection (SDGs: 1, 2, 6–9, 11–15), and inter-disci-
plinary actions (relational SDGs: 3, 4, 10–14, 16, 17). Regarding climate
change and climate risk, there is one goal directly focused on climate
issues – SDG13, although climate-related challenges are also incorpo-
rated into other related goals. Estimates indicate that implementing the
SDGs requires investments of USD 5–7 trillion annually. It is also noted
that the annual financing gap for the Sustainable Development Goals
reaches USD 2.5 trillion, with capital market managers managing assets
worth approximately USD 300 trillion each year.[1]

The SDGs are scheduled to be implemented by 2030, and financial
resources are required to achieve them. It is already known that there
is a problem with the so-called financial gap at the level of developing countries. The role of financial markets – which provide capital to
finance sustainable projects but also offer solutions such as sustainable
financial products and services supporting sustainable development – is
crucial in covering this financial gap. Regardless of the sources of funds
for financing sustainable development (these funds may come from various sources, e.g., public and private, even efforts have been made and
financing mechanisms dedicated to the SDGs have been built), a coordi-
nated and unified approach to spending financial resources is necessary
to ensure the achievement of SDGs and eliminate financing of unsustainable actions/projects. In this respect, financial markets and public
finances face many challenges, including regarding reporting activities
for sustainable development, such asESG reporting, ESG risk management, and tolerable development risk, or such as an organization and
formal and legal framework to ensure sustainable development through
joint action of states and financial markets. The Sustainable Development
Goals that banks are mainly focused on are those related to economic
growth and decent work (SDG8), climate action (SDG13), clean energy
(SDG7), sustainable cities and communities (SDG11), and responsible
consumption and production (SDG12). It should be noted that decision-
makers accountable for financial markets have a comprehensive impact
on the possibilities of implementing the SDGs, which is reflected in
their direct and indirect actions. Immediate actions concern financing
for implementing the SDGs or, more broadly, mobilizing capital for sustainable funding. As part of the cooperation formed with clients, financial institutions are entitled to determine the terms of such cooperation,
taking into account the principles of partnership, ethics, and good business practices, and within the framework of the conditions dictated by
the competitive market. The terms of cooperation between the financial

institution and the business sector depend on many factors, including the type of client, scope of collaboration, risk, and profitability. When setting transaction risk assessment criteria, financial institutions select entities, excluding those that do not meet the requirements for the availability of financial services. On the other hand, entities meeting the criteria, depending on the assessment of the transaction risk level, conditioned by the degree of fulfillment of the standard, are differentiated by financial institutions in terms of the conditions for using the services (e.g., price, scope of services, level of monitoring, legal collaterals, etc.). Therefore, transaction risk assessment changes under the influence of economic changes. It is evident in the conditions of "greening" the economy and social inclusion. These two phenomena referring to the environmental and social pillars of sustainable development strongly weigh on the need to extend the risk assessment criteria by financial institutions to include ESG risk and thus determine the role of financial institutions in support-ing the sustainable transformation of economies. Financial institutions are crucial in shifting enterprises' business models towards sustainable ones. However, the impact varies by business sector and financial system model. The financial model determines the form of cooperation between financial institutions and companies in financing adaptation activities to the requirements of sustainable development.

So far, several research results have been conducted and published on the SDGs considered in various contexts. Most of the research has been published in the form of articles. Those published in the form of monographs concerned the implementation of the SDGs in Europe and other parts of the world, legal aspects related to the implementation of the SDGs, the relationships between the SDGs, the impact of the SDGs on income inequality, and the SDGs and intellectual property. Relatively few titles on the publishing market concern the context and relationship between financial markets and, frankly, finance and the SDGs. Typically, the financial context appears as the amounts necessary to implement the SDGs in developed and developing countries or statistics of funds spent so far on the implementation of individual SDGs.

This monograph aims to show the role of financial markets in imple-menting and ensuring the SDGs. The monograph chapters present the SDGs' issues through the prism of implementation challenges and actions taken on financial markets to support the SDGs. The broader context of considerations is rarely taken up, and there is a significant research gap in the field of research and its results regarding, among oth-ers, considering financial markets as a factor stimulating activities under individual SDGs, including achieving the targets planned for them. It should be emphasized that the financial market is created by sectors and financial institutions offering several sustainable products supporting the achievement of the SDGs through direct financing and influencing entrepreneurs and their financial decisions. This monograph has been planned in such a way as to comprehensively show the role of financial markets in the implementation of the SDGs, with particular emphasis on the banking sector, the insurance sector, and the capital market. Much attention was also paid to the SDGs themselves, sustainable development, and ESG risk as factors that strongly interact and are interconnected. The monograph consists of seven chapters, including an introduction.

This chapter, the introduction, presents a justification for taking up the issue of the SDGs in terms of connections with the financial market and the importance of the financial market for achieving the SDGs. The research gap is justified, and the importance and need for conducting research and publishing results on the role of financial institutions and markets in implementing the SDGs are indicated. Potential groups of readers are also shown, especially those interested in the issues discussed in the monograph.

Chapter 2 presents the genesis of the 2030 Agenda along with measuring the implementation of the SDGs and the interactions between them, indicating critical points and measurement challenges aimed at implementing sustainable development. The chapter points out that sustainability is a concept that emerged in connection with the growing awareness of the looming ecological crisis. It aims to eliminate preventively or at least mitigate the differences between economic growth and social development, socio-economic development, and the natural environment. The emergence of concerns about the harmful effects of large-scale modern technologies on the environment can be traced back to the 1960s. However, the discussion about the development concept, which considers economic, social, and environmental aspects, began in the 1970s and 1980s. The reflections presented in Chapter 2 show that sustainable development has achieved remarkable popularity and has become the subject of extensive literature, including articles, books, analyses, legal regulations, and widespread discussions and debates on television and radio programs via Internet platforms. Although critical perspectives on this concept are less frequently articulated and published, their existence is undeniable. There were disappointments at the 2002 Earth Summit in Johannesburg when it became clear that the development goals set two years earlier at the Millennium Summit would still need to be achieved.

It led to initial doubts about the feasibility of the sustainable development strategy and a general decline in public interest in this concept. The chapter further presents the indicators related to sustainable development and SDGs. The chapter considers that eleven Headline Indicators exist, crucial in monitoring overarching objectives tied to the key challenges outlined in the Sustainable Development Strategy. The second level of the pyramid consists of 31 Operational Indicators related to operational objectives. In comparison, the third level includes 84 Explanatory Indicators, which further specify and detail the activities relevant to the operational indicators. Additionally, there is a category of contextual indicators. These indicators are not directly used to monitor the strategy's objectives, and they may be challenging to interpret in a normative way. The chapter also considers that the European Commission has introduced a comprehensive set of indicators for the EU's sustainable development goals, accessible through the Eurostat database. These indicators form the foundation for evaluating sustainable development across diverse domains.

Chapter 3 aims to indicate the relationships between financial markets and financial institutions operating within them and sustainability, ESG, and SDGs, indicating critical points and challenges for finance resulting from activities aimed at adapting to sustainability. The ongoing demographic, climate, and socio-economic changes have a financial dimension and create a new type of risk, ESG risk, which is currently one of the most significant from the perspective of the assessment and functioning of banking and financial institutions. It applies in particular to types of risk, such as environmental and reputational risks. Contemporary economics is, therefore, influenced by several factors that determine the need to implement changes and innovative solutions in finance. An attempt to increase the adjustment of finance to the expectations of sustainable growth and development is its "greening;" more broadly, sustainability is perceived as ensuring the equivalence of decision-making criteria (economic, social, and environmental) in decision-making processes in finance. It is in line with the postulates and concept of the SDGs. Green, responsible, sustainable finance is one of the most dynamically developing subdisciplines supporting SDGs. The chapter explains how sustainability risk and ESG risk impact financial markets and what the consequences of that impact are. The chapter presents initiatives and actions taken by the financial sector to adjust to sustainability requirements; however, the risk that the financial industry will not implement sustainability practices and that mitigating sustainability risk requires instruments and a legal and organizational framework, led to the new, sustainable finance paradigm being evolved. Financial markets are transforming, stimulated by the impact of sustainability. The chapter points out that ESG factors are gaining importance, mainly because of ESG risk and the development of ESG reporting. Non-financial reporting is crucial because it shows several threats and the possibilities of overcoming them (including in the context of taxation). The chapter concludes the role of financial markets and institutions is vital for catching the green and blue waves as providers of credit and financial resources that must decide where to invest and consider different risk factors. The chapter explains that it is worth paying attention to the following critical points when analyzing the challenges facing finance and financial markets in funding the SDGs. Currently, the issues of concern include gaps in financing, the low diversity in financing with a high concentration of funds primarily for improving energy efficiency, the lack of a theoretical framework and definitions, financing opportunities based on conventional sources, non-bankable projects, and the lack of an established effective financial mechanism for the SDGs. Financial markets are subject to regulations, including regulations regarding ESG. Hence, the approach of markets and institutions differs in individual countries. The European Union is currently the most advanced when it comes to the standardization of ESG requirements and regulations. Hence, financial institutions, including the ECB and EBA, propose specific definitional and regulatory solutions and standards.

Chapter 4 discusses the role of banks in achieving the SDG goals, indicating the factors causing differences and limitations. The chapter explains that following the announcement of the SDGs in 2015 and the adoption of the Paris Climate Agreement, sustainable development has become a priority for many countries, and the main challenge is securing financing for its implementation. International organizations, governments, central banks, and regulators have intensified their efforts to build a sustainable financial system, as well as to normalize and coordinate the activities of banks and provide financing for regional or national sustainable development strategies. They have set standards, formulated guidelines, issued recommendations, and ultimately shaped best practices at global, regional, national, and individual bank levels. The chapter points out that the European Union has dedicated two specific strategies to sustainable development: the European Green Deal and the strategy to finance the transition to a sustainable economy. Two action plans have also been developed: the Action Plan: Financing Sustainable

Growth and the European Green Deal Investment Plan. The EU leads the environmental, social, and governance regulatory movement with most ESG-related issues. The chapter explains that banks play a dual role in achieving the SDGs: as direct implementers of the goals and as supporters of goal achievement. Supporting the implementation of the SDGs requires both internal (appropriate adaptation of business models) and external actions resulting from stakeholder expectations. The chapter discusses how banks can contribute to achieving the SDGs. In particular, the chapter points out that banks need to be more efficient in managing the resources necessary for their business (e.g., through economical use of energy, water, paper, fuel, toner, etc.) by reducing their greenhouse gas emissions; conduct waste management, technological and organizational innovation, respect for human and labor rights or the creation of appropriate working conditions. Achieving the SDGs within a bank's operations is an essential prerequisite for promoting these goals among customers and building relationships with external stakeholders (e.g., through social engagement and philanthropic activities aimed at education and financial inclusion, as well as engagement in multi-stakeholder partnerships for the SDGs). The extraordinary influence of banks on the SDGs is expressed through the mitigation of ESG risks. By managing these risks, banks can strengthen their loan and investment portfolios and mitigate them for customers and consumers. The SDGs will be achieved by sustainable banking services and products that enable attracting and leveraging the savings of the population and businesses, as well as redirecting private investments towards ventures that attain the Sustainable Development Goals. The chapter concludes that banks have a much more significant impact on achieving the SDGs through their financial activities than through their internal processes. However, the reports primarily focus on the organization's internal resources and community engagement (CSR). It is rare for banks to disclose negative impacts on the SDGs, apart from mandatory disclosures (e.g., EU Taxonomy, SFRD). Based on the reported data, it is difficult to make an objective assessment of banks' commitment to achieving the SDGs due, among other things, to the descriptive nature of many indicators, which also have different information capacities, such as the use of inconsistent measurement principles and methods, estimated quantities or even units of measurement (e.g., paper consumption measured in sheets, flutes or kilograms). The lack of comparability also applies to rating agencies' assessments, which use different methods to assess banks' sustainable commitment. In addition, numerous rankings and competitions result in multiple banks reporting that they are leaders in sustainable banking. The rankings are created according to different criteria , which results in a bank being at the top of one ranking, coming second in others, or even not appearing in the ranking.

Chapter 5 presents selected ESG regulations affecting the activities of insurance companies in the European Union, Great Britain, the USA, and Australia. The chapter explains that insurance companies have a certain peculiarity as part of the financial sector. The essence of their activity is to exchange unpredictable financial risks for a specific, fixed cash deposit. Insurance companies are obliged to ensure their solvency and the ability of their policyholders to pay out at any time and, therefore, to invest their funds conservatively. Insurance regulators impose capital requirements for investments depending on the value of the risk taken, assuming that the riskier the investment, the higher the capital requirement. The chapter illustrates that the insurance sector plays a significant role in helping individual countries achieve sustainable development goals in economic growth, social inclusion, and environmental protection. In the dimension of environmental protection, the insurance sector contributes to the implementation of sustainable development goals through the appropriate structure of assets and liabilities of individual insurance companies. In this dimension, insurers can influence the achievement of the following sustainable development goals: SDG6 (Clean Water and Sanitation), SDG12 (Responsible Consumption and Production), SDG 15 (Life on Land), SDG 7 (Affordable and Clean Energy), SDG 13 (Climate Action), SDG 14 (Life Below Water and No Poverty), SDG 1 (No Poverty), SDG 3 (Good Health and Well-Being), SDG 8 (Decent Work and Economic Growth), SDG 9 (Industry, Innovation and Infrastructure), and SDG 11 (Sustainable Cities and Communities). The activities of insurers contribute to better social inclusion by providing insurance to the most marginal social groups (including disabled people, young people, women, older adults, and the unemployed). In this dimension, the activities of insurance companies can have a positive impact on the implementation of such sustainable development goals as SDG 4 (Quality Education), SDG 5 (Gender Equality), SDG 10 (Reduced Inequalities), SDG 16 (Peace Justice and Strong Institutions), SDG 17 (Partnership for the Goals), SDG 1 (No Poverty), SDG 3 (Good Health and Well-Being), SDG 8 (Decent Work and Economic Growth), SDG 9 (Industry, Innovation and Infrastructure), and SDG 11 (Sustainable Cities and Communities). In the economic area, the activities of the insurance sector, directly and indirectly, contribute to the implementation of the following goals: SDG 2

(Zero Hunger), SDG 7 (Affordable and Clean Energy), SDG 13 (Climate Action), SDG 14 (Life Below Water), SDG 1 (No Poverty), SDG 3 (Good Health and Well-Being), SDG 8 (Decent Work and Economic Growth), SDG 9 (Industry, innovation and Infrastructure), SDG 11 (Sustainable Cities and Communities), SDG 5 (Gender Equality), SDG 10 (Reduced Inequalities), SDG 16 (Peace Justice and Strong Institutions), and SDG 17 (Partnership for the Goals).

Chapter 6 draws attention to the importance of the stock exchange as a tool for implementing sustainable development on capital markets and the issue of creating a capital market union. The chapter points out that sustainable capital markets, in particular, contribute to the achievement of SDGs such as SDG13 (Climate Action), SDG8 (Decent Work and Economic Growth), and SDG12 (Responsible Consumption and Production). The chapter explains the importance of a sustainable capital market growing yearly. The global market for sustainable finance (i.e., bonds, funds, and voluntary carbon markets) was estimated to be worth USD 5.8 trillion in 2022, and, importantly, investors see sustainable finance as a long-term strategy. Despite difficult macroeconomic conditions, investor interest in sustainable funds was still more significant than in traditional funds, and the value of the global sustainable funds market in 2022 was USD 2.5 trillion (United Nations Conference on Trade and Development, 2023). Analyzing the relationships between SDGs and the capital market, the following sustainable development goals may be mentioned: SDG 13 (Climate Action), SDG 8 (Decent Work and Economic Growth), and SDG 12 (Responsible Consumption and Production). Environmental protection projects are trendy, confirmed by the green bond market, which is growing yearly. Institutional investors show particular interest in supporting projects related to sustainable energy. The capital-intensive and long-term nature of investments in renewable energy sources corresponds to the maturity profiles of pension funds' liabilities (United Nations Conference on Trade and Development, 2023). United Nations Conference on Trade and Development (UNCTAD) data shows that more than two-thirds of reporting funds have declared that they will achieve net zero in their investment portfolios by 2050. To this end, they plan to phase out fossil fuels in favor of renewable energy sources. Capital markets can play an essential role in supporting the sustainable transformation of economic entities. Financing is sometimes even more needed by entities preparing or in the process of transformation to a more sustainable operating model, i.e., switching to low-emission production methods. The capital market can be a significant source of capital for transforming entities operating in the so-called "brown" industries. Not all business entities can afford to switch to more "ecological" forms of doing business, and the possibility of obtaining stable and long-term sources of financing in this area may become a key factor enabling the decarbonization of enterprises with high carbon dioxide emissions.

Chapter 7 aims to present challenges, prospects, and recommendations of financial markets in implementing obligations arising from the SDGs. The chapter presents initiatives and regulations determining changes in the financial markets toward implementing the SDG goals. The chapter explains that climate change is an essential factor of instability in the financial market due to the risk of losses, the need to incur costs of hedging against risk, or the impact of non-financial factors. The essential act for building the regulatory environment for financial markets was the United Nations Environment Program Financial Initiative (UNEP FI). The European Union influences positive changes in financial markets towards the implementation of the SDG goals through directives (as obligatory regulations for members, with a more significant impact), good practices, sets of guidelines, or recommendations (they create optional rules for member countries). The chapter discusses that new business models are accepted by potential investors in financial markets if they explain how the decisions they make reflect the interests of their stakeholders and the environment and if the strategy is related to the implementation of the SDG goals in the context of being in line with the idea of sustainable development. The chapter concludes that achieving the SDG goals of the Science Based Targets Initiative (SBTi) is essential, which has developed a net zero standard for companies to be consistent with Sustainable Development Goals. (Net-Zero, 2023). Implementing the set standard has at least four limitations. First, there has yet to be a consensus on the extent of climate impacts in terms of the types of greenhouse gases. Some companies refer to all greenhouse gases (GHG), others only specifically to CO_2 (Net Zero, 2023). There is also inconsistency regarding the scope of corporate activities to which the net-zero target applies. Third, significant differences exist in the implemented strategy to combat climate change. The fourth problem is the scope of the SDG goals (2050), and that the transition goals (so-called milestones) need to be defined. These four topics represent a severe limitation to the SDG goals and the implementation of ESG (Net Zero, 2023). Many financial institutions know the need to finance climate change, the opportunities that change brings, and the associated risks. Thanks to their support, efforts are being made to engage market participants and integrate ESG factors into mainstream financial practices. Financial institutions operating in financial markets are becoming catalysts in disclosing ESG information, encouraging or requiring reporting (over 80%). The leading role of these institutions in achieving green goals provides companies with a unique opportunity to develop effective transformation paths based on the standards of financial institutions and benchmarks of other financial market participants.

The monograph attempts to show how financial markets support or can support the implementation of the SDGs. In particular, attention was paid to the role of financial markets in ensuring direct financing of activities aimed at achieving the SDGs. Financial capital is a necessary condition for the full implementation of all SDGs, and the financial gap at the level of developing countries poses a particular challenge for decision-makers in closing the financial assembly and finding sources of financing. The role of indirect actions to implement the SDGs through financial markets is also essential – indirect activities concern customer segmentation and revising the business models of financial institutions towards sustainable business models. Financial markets can support the green transformation by financing green projects but also by influencing the behavior of market participants, including entrepreneurs, by defining cooperation requirements. It may already be observed the actions of financial institutions by excluding entrepreneurs from the so-called sectors from cooperation or offering enterprises from so-called "dirty sectors" higher prices for banking products and services due to a higher valuation of ESG risk. Financial markets also support projects and activities to improve the blue economy and ensure the spread of the so-called blue wave. Financial markets and institutions also support social goals and projects in this area: possible activities include financing charity activities, sponsoring funding scholarships for youth, or financing investment projects that directly support solving social problems such as exclusion, hunger, and poverty. An essential element of the considerations contained in the monograph are also those relating to the issues and challenges facing financial markets and institutions in terms of adapting to the requirements of sustainable development and the associated risks. In this respect, it is particularly worth paying attention to non-financial reporting, greenwashing, and the transformation of business models of financial institutions. The authors hope that the monograph will be a source of knowledge about the relationship between finance and the SDGs and will contribute to further research and discussion on the issues raised. Nowadays, ESG is a factor conditioning the initiation of transformation processes in financial markets, which is the transformation towards a green, blue, environmentally friendly, and socially oriented economy. This type of economy requires sustainable financial markets and the implementation of SDGs to complete the green transformation, inclusive growth, and sustainable development. Transformation processes are taking place in all financial markets, particularly banking, insurance, and capital markets. In banking, sustainability is expressed in green and responsible banking. However, all financial institutions already offer green and sustainable financial services. It supports the process of implementing SDGs and transformation towards sustainable economic development and responsible banking, implements the assumptions of social inclusion, and respects and disseminates ethical standards. SDGs are disseminated through financial institutions and instruments used within the financial markets. Sustainable finance supports the implementation of SDGs. Therefore, respecting the postulates of sustainable finance is also a challenge from the point of view of institutional economics. The organization of the financial markets, including the financial system, in terms of implementing SDGs requires several changes of a structural and organizational nature, as well as changes within the corporate culture of individual institutions and the mission of their operation. These changes should be orderly and controlled, which depends on the quality of regulation. Regulations are essential primarily from the point of view of shaping and supervising the offer of financial products and services, but also the security and stability of the banking and financial sector, which depends on the quality of risk management (including the approach to ESG risk).

The monograph is addressed to a wide range of recipients (readers), from scientists, teachers, politicians, and governments, to PhD and other students interested in the financial sector from the perspective of SDGs, sustainable finance, and financial markets and relationships between them, as well as to practitioners dealing with SDGs, ESG, and the financial market and finances as part of their professional work. The recipient group also includes people wanting to acquire or deepen their knowledge about the link between SDGs and financial markets, especially the banking, insurance, and capital markets. The authors believe that the recipients of the monograph can also include all people interested in expanding their knowledge of the role of financial markets and institutions in achieving the SDGs.

On behalf of all the authors,
Magdalena Ziolo

NOTE

1.   S. Dawson: *The role of financial services in helping to meet the UN Sustainable Development Goals*, https://eyfinancialservicesthoughtgallery.ie/un-sustainable-development-goals/ (Accessed: 5.01.2024).

2. Sustainable Development Goals (SDGs): Concept and measurement

Iwona Bąk

2.1 GENESIS AND RELEVANCE OF THE 2030 AGENDA FOR SUSTAINABLE DEVELOPMENT

Sustainability is a concept that has emerged in the context of growing awareness of the impending ecological crisis (Duran et al., 2015). Its objective has become to eliminate preventively, or at least mitigate, the disparities between economic growth and social development, and between socioeconomic development and the natural environment.

The genesis of concerns regarding the detrimental impacts of modern large-scale technologies on the environment can be traced back to the 1960s (Carson, 1962). However, the discussion on the concept of development considering not only economic but also social and environmental aspects began in the 1970s and 1980s (Meadows et al., 1972). Warnings about the dangers of environmental over-exploitation were articulated in 1967 in the U Thant report (Bąk and Cheba, 2018). These threats, especially those linked to natural resource depletion and ecosystem degradation, were also featured in the Club of Rome's 1972 report, "Limits to Growth" (Berger and Zwirner, 2008).

In 1972, a conference convened in Stockholm under the auspices of the United Nations entitled "We have only one Earth" with a specific focus on environmental issues. The primary outcome of this conference was the issuance of a declaration comprising 26 principles, which included the imperative to establish an environmental policy, emphasising that it should not be perceived as a hindrance to development. The Stockholm Declaration had no binding force, but its provisions were repeatedly referred to in the construction of international agreements. While the Stockholm Declaration did not possess binding authority, its principles were recurrently referenced in the formulation of international agreements. Within this declaration, for the first time, a part of the international community (with 77 countries voting in favour of the declaration) pledged to accord appropriate priority to environmental concerns.

During the 1980s, a new paradigm of sustainable development gained widespread recognition and application. The term "sustainable development" was officially introduced in 1982 by the United Nations General Assembly through the World Nature Charter. Subsequently, the United Nations (UN) appointed a panel of 22 experts from both developed and developing nations to delineate long-term environmental strategies for the international community. This panel, known as the World Commission on Environment and Development (WCED) or the Brundtland Commission, submitted a seminal report titled "Our Common Future" to the UN in 1987 (WCED 1987).

Brundtland's report centred on the fundamental requirements and welfare of individuals, emphasising the imperative of securing global equity for forthcoming generations through the equitable redistribution of resources to foster economic growth in less affluent nations, thereby enabling all individuals to fulfil their essential needs. The report strongly advocates the possibility of concurrently achieving social equity, economic advancement, and environmental sustainability, thereby underscoring the three fundamental pillars of sustainable development: the environment, the economy, and society. Moreover, it elucidates the necessity for holistic and sustainable resolutions to challenges related to population dynamics, agriculture and food security, biodiversity, energy alternatives, industrial practices, and other pertinent issues (Du Pisani, 2006).

From the Brundtland Report (WCED 1987) comes the most famous definition of the term sustainable development, according to which it is "development that meets the needs of the present without compromising the ability of future generations to meet their own needs". In accordance with the commitments made in Stockholm, a significant conference addressing environmental concerns was convened two decades later. In June 1992, the Earth Summit, officially known as the United Nations Conference on Environment and Development, was held in Rio de Janeiro, representing the largest gathering of its kind in history. Notably, this event placed significant emphasis on environmental issues, recognising their particular relevance for the world's most economically disadvantaged nations. The Earth Summit yielded several pivotal documents and conventions:

- The Rio Declaration on Environment and Development, signed by all participating countries (a total of 179 nations), encompasses 27 overarching principles, rights, and obligations designed to serve as the foundational framework for establishing novel international relations and societal dynamics.
- Agenda 21, comprising a comprehensive set of recommendations and actions for environmental safeguarding,
- The Convention on Climate Change, an obligatory agreement signed by 154 participating countries which mandates the signatory states must undertake measures aimed at mitigating the adverse impact of human activities on the environment. It formulates guidelines for international cooperation aimed at reducing greenhouse gas emissions.
- The Convention on the Conservation of Biodiversity, which emphasises the necessity of ensuring equitable protection for both fauna and flora.
- The Declaration of Principles of Cooperation for the Development, Protection, and Utilisation of All Forests.

The Kyoto Protocol on Greenhouse Gas Emissions was endorsed in December 1997, representing the inaugural supplementary agreement to the United Nations Framework Convention on Climate Change (UNFCCC). Its provisions encompass the commitments of industrialised nations to curtail the emission of greenhouse gases, recognised as major contributors to global warming (Tu, 2018; Kameyama, 2004). The primary objective of the Protocol entails a 5% reduction in greenhouse gas emissions during the period of 2008–2012 relative to the levels recorded in 1990.

Subsequently, in 2000, the United Nations Millennium Summit convened, addressing a spectrum of issues pertaining to conflict resolution, public health, and poverty eradication, compelling affluent nations to undertake measures aimed at enhancing living standards globally, particularly in the regions commonly referred to as Third World countries (McArthur, J.W., 2014; Kumar et al., 2016). During this summit, the Millennium Development Goals were adopted, encompassing the following objectives:

- eradicating extreme poverty and hunger,
- ensuring universal primary education,
- promotion of gender equality and the social advancement of women,
- reducing child mortality,
- improving maternal health care,
- curtailing the prevalence of HIV/AIDS, malaria, and other diseases,
- implementing sustainable methods for natural resource management,
- establishing a global partnership agreement for development.

In 2002, marking the tenth anniversary of the Rio Earth Summit, another significant United Nations conference was convened, this time in Johannesburg, often referred to as "Rio +10". The primary objective of this gathering was to scrutinise the validity of previously adopted assumptions regarding the implementation of sustainable development. It aimed to encapsulate the decade-long international community's endeavours, which were deemed somewhat ineffective in implementing the concept of sustainable development (Pring, 2002).

Following the established principle of organising Earth Summits every two decades, in June 2012, another global conference, Rio +20, was held in Rio de Janeiro. During this event, the Rio Earth Summit Declaration, titled "The Future We Want" (Noga and Wolbringa, 2013), was endorsed by 193 United Nations member states, encompassing environmental matters. Additionally, several economic, social, and environmental recommendations delineated in Agenda 21 were adopted.

In 2013, the inaugural meeting of the High-Level Panel on the Post-2015 Development Agenda, known as the High-Level Political Forum, took place. This forum served as the primary United Nations platform for sustainable development and replaced the Commission on Sustainable Development, which had been operational since 1993.

The culmination of the Open Working Group's endeavours to formulate new Sustainable Development Goals resulted in a document adopted at the Summit of Heads of State and Government in New York on 25–27 September 2015, under the title "Transforming Our World: The 2030 Agenda for Sustainable Development". The primary aim of the 2030 Agenda is to foster a just global society founded on the principles of legal adherence and inclusive governance. Its fundamental message underscores the pursuit of development that ensures a dignified existence for all inhabitants of the Earth, primarily through the eradication of all forms and dimensions of poverty, including extreme poverty, and ensuring peace. The new program comprises 17 goals (see Figure 2.1) and delineates 169 targets to be accomplished within a 15-year timeframe, addressing critical aspects for both humanity and the planet, encompassing population, planet, prosperity, peace, and partnership.

The concept of sustainable development has garnered remarkable popularity and has become the subject of extensive literature, including articles, books, analyses, and legal regulations, as well as widespread discussions and debates in television and radio broadcasts and across internet platforms. Although critical perspectives on this concept are less frequently articulated and published, their existence is undeniable. Feelings of disappointment had already emerged at the 2002 Earth Summit in Johannesburg when it became evident that the development goals established two years earlier at the Millennium Summit would remain unattained. This marked the onset of initial doubts regarding the feasibility of implementing the sustainable development strategy, leading to a general waning of public interest in this concept.

Despite the political correctness associated with the concept of sustainable development, it has faced criticism from both radical and conservative factions. Less developed countries have expressed suspicion that sustainable development is an ideology imposed by affluent industrialised nations to enforce stricter conditions and aid regulations on developing nations. Concerns persist that sustainable development may inadvertently perpetuate the economic disparities between developed and underdeveloped countries (Mitcham, 1995).

It is widely recognised that the achievement of the programme, which consists of 17 Sustainable Development Goals (SDGs) and 169 related targets, requires efforts at national, regional, and local levels in all sectors of society (Schmidt-Trauba et al., 2017). To some, the SDGs represent an opportunity to amalgamate the development initiatives of diverse sectors into a unified programme (Eurostat, 2015). Conversely, there are apprehensions regarding the 2030 Agenda for Sustainable Development being overly expansive, consequently posing challenges in terms of measurement and management. Acknowledging the interconnectedness and interdependence of all 17 SDGs is pivotal in the pursuit of their attainment, demanding a transformation of policy into practice.

SUSTAINABLE DEVELOPMENT GOALS

Source: United Nations, 2015.

2.2 MEASURING THE IMPLEMENTATION OF THE SUSTAINABLE DEVELOPMENT GOALS

The Sustainable Development Goals represent a collection of concrete and quantifiable objectives for national development. The international community evaluates these objectives through the use of indicators derived from available data and various methodological studies. Consequently, to advance the progress toward the realisation of the 2030 Agenda, it is imperative to have access to high-quality data that can be compared over time (Nilashi et al., 2023). Low-quality, outdated, or incomplete data can lead to erroneous decision-making. Nevertheless, it is important to note that official statistics alone may not encompass all the data essential for comprehensively framing the indicators for the Sustainable Development Goals (Fraisl et al., 2022). It poses a formidable challenge, given that the SDGs must be measurable, grounded in the latest research, and applicable to both developed and developing nations (Griggs et al., 2013).

Sustainable development indicators and their systems must adhere to a set of critical criteria, as outlined by Dobrzańska (2007):

- comprehensive and equitable reflection of the fundamental dimensions of cultural, economic, and ecological permanence (or impermanence), encompassing the interrelationships among these dimensions;
- scientific justification;
- simple design and ease of interpretation;
- appropriate sensitivity, enabling the demonstration of developmental trends;
- inclusion of a threshold (reference value) to assess the disparity between the current state and the desired state, thereby distinguishing impermanence from permanence;
- reliance on widely-accepted standards;
- accessibility of information with a reasonable cost–benefit ratio;
- adequate data quality;
- regular updates according to reliable procedures;
- openness to verification and improvement in response to evolving human needs, advancements in the understanding of sustainable development, progress in science, technological innovations, and enhanced measurement capabilities.

Sustainability indicators can be structured using a hierarchical framework, often represented as a "pyramid" (Eurostat, 2015). This framework categorises these indicators into three distinct levels, creating a stratified system (Figure 2.2). At the apex of the pyramid, there exist 11 Headline Indicators, which assume a crucial role in the monitoring of overarching objectives tied to the key challenges outlined in the Sustainable Development Strategy. The second level of the pyramid consists of 31 Operational Indicators, which are related to operational objectives, while the third level includes 84 Explanatory Indicators, which further specify and detail the activities relevant to the operational indicators.

The set of indicators also encompasses those that are currently in the process of development, serving to enhance and provide a more comprehensive illustration of progress. These include indicators under development, which are anticipated to attain suitable quality standards within a two-year timeframe. Examples of such indicators may involve the generation of hazardous waste categorised by type of economic activity, public expenditure on education, and child welfare. They also include indicators earmarked for long-term development ("indicators to be developed"), such as eco-innovation, green public procurement, expenditure on research and development relevant to sustainable development, and employment within the sector of green goods and services.

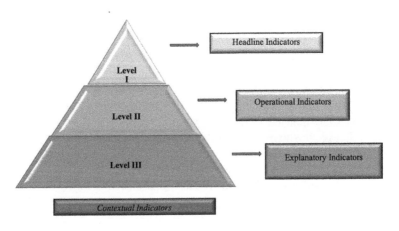

Source: Źródło: Eurostat, 2015.

Figure 2.2   Hierarchical structure of sustainable development indicators published by Eurostat

The European Commission developed a set of indicators in 2017 to monitor the SDGs within the context of the European Union (EU), in accordance with Communication COM(2016) 739, 'Next steps toward a sustainable future for Europe'. This set of indicators forms the foundation for Eurostat's annual monitoring report on the progress of SDGs in the EU, enhancing statistical quality and ensuring consistent monitoring of the EU Sustainable Development Goals. The construction of the EU SDG indicator set adheres to the following principles (EU, 2023):

- grounded in the 17 Sustainable Development Goals, the indicator set maintains a balanced representation across the social, economic, environmental, and institutional dimensions of sustainable development, as stipulated in the text of Agenda 2030 for each objective;
- limited to a maximum of 6 indicators per objective, the indicator set ensures equal emphasis on all objectives while keeping the total set of indicators to around 100. This figure is widely acknowledged as the upper limit for effective and standardised reporting, as recommended by experts from the National Statistical Offices, OECD, Eurostat, and other institutions;
- incorporating multi-purpose indicators (MPIs) that serve the monitoring of multiple targets. As a result, each target is monitored using a total of 7 to 11 indicators within the current set;
- the addition of new indicators involves the removal of existing indicators within the same objective. New indicators are introduced only if they enhance the measurement of progress towards the SDGs within the EU context. These potential new indicators must be fully developed ('ready to use') and demonstrate enhanced policy relevance and/or superior statistical quality compared to the current indicator;
- the selection of new indicators must align with the criteria for policy relevance, admissibility requirements, and quality assessment established for the EU SDG indicator set.

Table 2.1 provides a detailed set of EU SDG indicators set out in the 2023 SDG Monitoring Report and all review developments for 2023. The published database (EU, 2023) includes 33 multi-purpose indicators (MPIs), which are indicators primarily associated with one goal but are also utilised for monitoring other goals. This approach facilitates the examination of interconnections between various goals, resulting in each

Table 2.1   Statistical summary of the main characteristics of the 2023 EU SDG indicator set

Goals	Total	MPIs	Select Indicators, of which			New Indicators	Indicators adjusted	Indicators on hold
			Annual frequency	Provider Eurostat	In UN list			
No poverty	6	+3	6	6	5			1
Zero hunger	5	+3	4	4	1			2
Good health and well-being	6	+5	5	5	3			2
Quality education	6		4	5	5		1	
Gender equality	6	+2	5	3	5		1	
Clean water and sanitation	6	+1	4	2	5		1	2
Affordable and clean energy	6		6	6	3			
Decent work and economic growth	6	+3	6	6	4			1
Industry, innovation and infrastructure	6	+3	6	5	5			
Reduced inequalities	6	+5	6	6	4			1

Goals	Total	MPIs	Select Indicators, of which			New Indicators	Indicators adjusted	Indicators on hold
			Annual frequency	Provider Eurostat	In UN list			
Sustainable cities and communities	6	+3	3	4	5	1	2	2
Responsible consumption and production	6	+1	5	5	2	1	1	3
Climate action	5	+2	5		3			2
Life below water	6		5		4		1	
Life on land	6	+2	3	1	5			3
Peace, justice and strong institutions	6		5	3	5		2	
Partnership for the goals	6		6	3	4			
Total	100	+33	84	64	68	2	9	19
Compared to 2022 version	-1	+2	-5	+1	+1	-	-	-

Source: Źródło: EU, 2023.

objective being monitored using six to eleven different indicators. The majority of these indicators are updated on an annual basis (84 indicators), although 16 indicators receive less frequent updates.

The European Commission has introduced a comprehensive set of indicators for the EU Sustainable Development Goals, which are accessible through the Eurostat database. These indicators form the foundation for evaluating the state of sustainable development across diverse domains. The extensive array of indicators underscores the intricate nature of sustainability (Alaimo et al., 2021), emphasising that each indicator is significant and should not be examined in isolation but instead in conjunction with the others (Maggino, 2017).

The assessment of the implementation of the sustainable development concept has garnered significant attention from both theorists and practitioners (Golding et al., 2017; Schmidt-Traub et al., 2017). According to Büyüközkan and Karabulut (2018), "sustainability performance assessment models should be more sustainable, relevant criteria and their interrelationships should be well defined, and account should be taken of the subjectivity of the qualitative criteria inherent in sustainability indicators." As a consequence, issues related to the selection of appropriate indicators and the choice of analytical methods for conducting multidimensional comparative analyses in the face of the complexity of development challenges are gaining prominence. Efforts are being made to integrate sustainability indicators through the utilisation of multi-criteria techniques (Munda, 2008; Huang et al., 2011; Ture et al., 2019; Zinatizadeh et al., 2017; Dos Santos et al., 2019; Roszkowska and Filipowicz-Chomko, 2020). The outcome is a proliferation of diverse measurement approaches, accompanied by numerous adaptations, often influenced by various international policies, contributing to the multiplicity and intricacy of the assessment methods (Bąk and Cheba, 2020).

2.3   INTERACTIONS BETWEEN THE SUSTAINABLE DEVELOPMENT GOALS

The Sustainable Development Goals (SDGs) are inherently multidimensional and intricately interconnected. Advancements toward one goal are inextricably linked through intricate feedback mechanisms with other goals (van Soest et al., 2019), with efforts directed at one goal having positive and negative consequences for other goals. A pressing research priority concerning the SDGs revolves around the quantitative analysis of these interrelations among the different SDGs. This analysis serves to elucidate the nature of these interactions and offers decision-makers more in-depth insights (Scherer et al., 2018; Pham-Truffert et al., 2020; Sompolska-Rzechuła and Kurdyś-Kujawska, 2021).

In order to comprehensively analyse the interactions of the Sustainable Development Goals (SDGs), it is imperative to identify synergies and trade-offs. When a significant positive correlation exists between a pair of SDG indicators, it is categorised as a synergy, whereas a significant negative correlation is labelled as a trade-off. By evaluating these synergies and trade-offs on both a global and national scale, the most prevalent interactions between SDGs can be identified. Research conducted by Warchold et al. (2020) has further demonstrated that SDG interactions vary depending on factors such as income, region, country, gender, age, and population location.

The first comprehensive quantitative analysis of synergies and trade-offs within and between the SDGs was conducted by Pradhan et al. (2017). According to their findings, the majority of countries exhibit a prevalence of positive correlations over negative ones among pairs of indicators associated with specific SDGs. For instance, the authors highlight the case of SDG1, focused on the eradication of poverty, which displays synergistic linkages with several other SDGs, including SDG3 (good health and well-being), SDG4 (quality of education), SDG5 (gender equality), SDG6 (clean water and sanitation) and SDG10 (reduction of inequalities). Additionally, progress in SDG3 (good health and well-being) is mainly in line with progress in SDG1 (poverty reduction), SDG4 (quality of education), SDG5 (gender equality), SDG6 (clean water and sanitation) and SDG10 (inequality reduction).

In contrast, SDG12, which pertains to responsible consumption, reveals trade-offs with several SDGs, including SDG10 (reduction of inequalities), SDG1 (eradication of poverty), SDG6 (clean water and sanitation), SDG3 (good health and well-being), SDG4 (quality of education), SDG5 (gender equality), and SDG2 (zero hunger).

Other scholars have undertaken similar research efforts. Rocha et al. (2019) observed that healthier lifestyles and improved access to medical assistance tend to be more prevalent in larger cities, aligning with the objectives of SDG 3, which emphasises "Good health and well-being." Paradoxically, in these larger urban areas, despite a higher incidence of non-communicable diseases, the occurrence of related deaths is relatively less frequent.

Brelsford et al. (2017) revealed that larger cities exhibit enhanced economic productivity, in harmony with the aims of SDG8, which promotes "Decent work and economic growth". However, these urban centres also present environmental challenges, as reflected in SDG13 ("Climate action"), SDG14 ("Life under water"), and SDG15 ("Life on land"). Moreover, larger cities tend to experience increased inequality, as indicated by the objectives of SDG10, which focuses on "Reducing inequality".

Fader et al. (2018) introduced a quantitative approach aimed at assessing the potential trade-offs and synergies among sustainability goals concerning water, food, and energy. Their analysis revealed varying dynamics: certain objectives demonstrated mutual support, while others exhibited no interaction, and some goals were found to be conflicting. For instance, objectives 2.5 (focused on maintaining genetic diversity), 6.5 (pertaining to integrated water management implementation), and 7.a (concerned with strengthening international cooperation for clean energy access) demonstrated no conflict with other objectives and displayed different levels of synergy with the majority of the remaining objectives.

Conversely, the diverse objectives within SDG2, particularly goal 2.b (the rectification and prevention of trade restrictions), indicate limited harmony with other objectives, potentially resulting in the overuse of resources required for other purposes or posing a threat to ecosystem services. Furthermore, their research substantiates the widely held belief that SDG6 (water) exhibits the highest number of potential synergies, totalling 124. Consequently, the accomplishment of water-related objectives would consistently facilitate the achievement of other interconnected goals.

Nerini et al. (2018) investigated the trade-offs and synergies associated with SDG7, which is dedicated to clean and accessible energy, and its interplay with other SDGs. Akuraju et al. (2020), in their research focused on sub-Saharan cities, exploring the interactions between SDG11 (Sustainable Cities and Communities) and SDG6 (Clean Water and Sanitation). Their findings underscored the significance of decentralised water management as an integral component of sustainable cities, particularly in terms of providing access to clean water.

Moyer and Bohl (2019) identified three distinct pathways of development, encompassing technology, lifestyle changes, and decentralised management, each offering potential routes to achieving the Sustainable Development Goals associated with social development. Yang et al. (2020) delved into an examination of how experts from different countries perceive and prioritise the Sustainable Development Goals while also exploring their linkages to environmental risks. In a separate study,

Wang et al. (2022) undertook an assessment of the interactions between the Sustainable Development Goals in the context of water contamination with nutrients in China. Their findings revealed a total of 319 interactions between the SDGs related to clean water (SDG6 and SDG14) and other SDGs, comprising 286 positive interactions (synergies) and 33 negative interactions (trade-offs).

In a study conducted by Egbende et al. (2023), the interactions between the Sustainable Development Goals and health in the Democratic Republic of the Congo (DRC) were thoroughly examined. Their findings revealed that SDG16, focusing on "Peace, Justice and Strong Institutions," exerted the most substantial impact on other goals and was recognised as a key priority for the DRC's pursuit of the SDGs. Moreover, the research demonstrated that advancements toward SDG3, which pertains to "Good Health and Well-being," were instrumental in promoting progress toward the majority of the SDGs, with positive feedback observed through second-order interactions. Furthermore, progress in achieving the other SDGs was identified as contributing to the progress of SDG3, particularly concerning "Good Health and Quality of Life." Notably, SDG16 emerged as having the highest positive potential when second-order interactions were considered. These results underscore the significance of acknowledging the synergies and trade-offs that exist in the interactions between health and other SDGs.

Omer and Noguchi (2020) explored the complexity of the interaction between building materials and sustainability goals, aiming to establish a knowledge-based system to support decision-makers, designers, and stakeholders in the construction industry in implementing Agenda 2030. This research proved that building materials can contribute significantly to the achievement of 13 goals and 25 targets of SDGs. The framework showed that the direct positive contribution of building materials on the SDGs has been noticed in SDG 3, SDG 7, SDG 9, SDG 11, SDG 12, SDG 13, and SDG 15, while an invisible contribution has been shown in SDG 2, SDG 5, SDG 10, and SDG 16. Coopman et al. (2016) developed a conceptual framework based on a systematic and comprehensive literature review coupled with critical content analysis. Their framework aimed to enhance the understanding of the reciprocal relationships between the SDGs in developed countries, with a particular focus on the interlinkages between SDG 12 (Sustainable Consumption and Production) and other SDGs.

Osborn et al. (2015) emphasised that different countries will face varying challenges in pursuing the Sustainable Development Goals (SDGs), with the level of challenge determined by the country's existing development conditions. Factors such as a country's economic and urban development play a pivotal role in shaping its capacity to progress towards sustainable development. On the other hand, Hellden et al. (2022) consider the synergy of the Sustainable Development Goals (SDGs) to be an effective approach for policymakers to gain a systemic understanding of how sustainability shapes both human health and well-being and, reciprocally, how these factors impact the SDGs. They perceive the SDGs as an integrated and interdependent system of objectives, highlighting their direct and indirect influence on one another. Despite this explicit acknowledgement of indivisibility in the preamble of Agenda 2030, the document itself lacks specific guidance on how to identify, characterise, and manage synergies and trade-offs between the goals.

While the 17 SDGs provide policymakers with a widely accepted and socially inclusive framework for understanding the multifaceted dimensions of sustainability, there remains a dearth of an accessible and intuitive approach for assessing the interactions between these objectives and identifying their potential for synergies or trade-offs. Conventional political discourse surrounding the SDGs has often been confined to a binary view, categorising interactions as either advantageous or detrimental to a specific policy objective. In contrast, the researchers sought to transcend this binary perspective by evaluating interactions among sustainability goals, focusing on a limited number of goals or a single policy area and their interrelation with the SDGs.

In recent years, a wide range of methodologies and approaches have been employed, spanning modelling tools to document analysis, in order to delve into the intricacies of the interconnections between the Sustainable Development Goals, primarily with the aim of ensuring policy coherence (Allen et al., 2016). The pursuit of the SDGs presents a significant challenge for all nations, necessitating the establishment of an advanced and resolute national system that will enhance the demand for technology, innovation, and resources to construct such a system (Omer and Noguchi, 2020). Analysing the interactions between selected goals or tasks allows for the creation of a matrix that depicts not only pairwise interactions but also the broader direct influence that the focal goal has on the encompassed set of goals or tasks and vice versa. Employing network analysis, for instance, enables the identification of clusters of closely interrelated goals or objectives, as well as those that seem to be relatively unaffected by progress in achieving other goals or tasks (Hellden et al., 2022). Such an approach can be valuable in guiding the coordination of cooperation among entities representing various goals. Furthermore, international exchanges and collaboration between countries and entities can serve as a means to facilitate "capacity building" (Leal Filho et al., 2020).

2.4 EMERGING MEASUREMENT CHALLENGES AND FURTHER REFLECTIONS

By setting the Sustainable Development Goals (SDGs), countries around the world have agreed to a prosperous, socially inclusive, and environmentally sustainable future for all. However, this ambitious vision reveals a critical gap in scientific insights, namely how to achieve the 17 SDGs simultaneously. Utilising the 169 related targets and 232 indicators designated for monitoring the implementation of the Sustainable Development Goals can prove challenging due to their sheer volume, broad scope, lack of structure, and occasional absence of quantification. Addressing a spectrum of pressing global concerns, including poverty, inequality, climate change, environmental degradation, peace, and justice, the SDGs demand an integrated approach.

Nunes et al. (2016) underscore that despite the United Nations' adoption of the Sustainable Development Goals, there exists a deficiency in a framework that facilitates their integrated operationalisation. Nevertheless, the implementation of such a comprehensive and diverse program poses challenges to policies and practices at the national, regional, and local levels across all sectors of society. There is a particular need to integrate strategies and approaches to operationalising the SDGs in a manner that emphasises their interdependence and offers explicit indicators and measures of their attainment.

As noted by some authors (Moyer and Hedden, 2020), the world is currently not on course to meet a significant number of the Sustainable Development Goals pertaining to social development, and the progress made between 2015 and 2030 is anticipated to be limited. In fact, it is expected that certain countries will fall short of fully attaining any of the targets within this domain. Projections suggest that by 2030, only 63% of the SDG targets can be achieved, with this figure increasing to 89% by 2050. The authors have drawn attention to the particular challenges associated with reaching specific SDG indicators, such as access to safe sanitation facilities, completion of upper secondary education, and addressing underweight children. These challenges signify enduring developmental issues that require substantial changes in both national and international aid policies and prioritisation. Furthermore, the authors have pinpointed 28 countries that are particularly vulnerable and not expected to achieve any of the nine social development targets. According to their perspective, international aid should be directed toward these nations.

Moyer and Bohl (2019) propose three alternative policy approaches to attain the Sustainable Development Goals (SDGs): technology adoption, lifestyle modification, and decentralised management. They emphasise the significance of considering the geographical scale when evaluating progress towards the SDGs. While many of these goals appear feasible when assessed at a global level, the results are less optimistic when evaluated on a country-by-country basis, particularly for smaller and less affluent nations. Consequently, it is crucial to prioritise these least developed countries in global endeavours to enhance sustainable social development. Notably, in Africa, the target values are met in only 9% of countries for sanitation indicators, 7% for lower secondary school graduation, and 5% for addressing underweight children (Moyer and Hedden, 2020).

Failing to attain the SDGs is likely to have detrimental consequences for billions of people worldwide, leading to severe livelihood disruption, increased poverty, and the spread of diseases. The most vulnerable populations, predominantly residing in developing countries, will bear the brunt of these repercussions (Leal Filho et al., 2020). Numerous studies have explored the challenges and prospects related to the Sustainable Development Goals (Moyer and Bohl, 2019; Yang et al., 2020). Some scholars and practitioners have noted the inherent difficulty in achieving these goals due to their multifaceted nature (Horton, 2014).

Leal Filho et al. (2020) have identified several critical barriers to achieving Sustainable Development Goals, which include:

- unclear goals: some goals lack clear explanations, allowing for individual interpretation and hindering effective implementation;
- difficulties related to collaborative efforts: ensuring cooperation among multiple stakeholders to achieve common goals can be challenging;
- compromises: conflicts may arise between different objectives, necessitating the identification of compromises when achieving one goal may require sacrificing another;
- accountability for commitments made to the SDGs;

- financial constraints: substantial financial investments are required to achieve these goals, posing a significant barrier, especially for underdeveloped countries;
- capacity building: acquiring the necessary skills, tools, and education for task execution to achieve the goals can be challenging, often due to financial constraints;
- technology and data: successfully pursuing the goals demands extensive data collection and trend monitoring, which, in turn, relies on up-to-date technology that is not always readily available;
- culture: cultural norms and values may inhibit individuals from embracing new ideas and development.

Achieving the Sustainable Development Goals will require a fundamental transformation of contemporary societies. Stafford-Smith et al. (2017) emphasise the importance of addressing interlinkages within three key areas: between sectors (such as finance, agriculture, energy, and transport), among social actors (including local authorities, government agencies, the private sector, and civil society), and across low, middle, and high-income countries. The authors propose seven recommendations to enhance these connections at both global and national levels:

1. Capacity building: universal literacy in system approaches
2. Data and monitoring: essential sustainable development variables
3. Technology: integrated global innovation system for SD products and services
4. Governance: integrated development plans overseen by high-level ministries
5. Partnerships: focused around SDGs as a Common Standards package
6. Trade: Facilitated trade in products and services for SD
7. Finance: support for SD product and service market development in lower-income countries.

Enhancing the quality of existing data plays a pivotal role in making informed decisions regarding the SDGs. While criteria for assessing data quality at both international and national levels exist, their practical implementation in assessing specific SDGs is still in its early stages. The Inter-Agency Expert Group on the Sustainable Development Goals (IAEG-SDG) is progressively refining the methodology and availability of data on the SDGs. However, the financial and technical capacities of many countries' organisations and statistical units fall short of the requirements for different SDGs.

The absence of comprehensive data presents a significant challenge to accurately measuring the progress of SDG implementation and making informed organisational decisions. Furthermore, incomplete data can hamper the accurate prediction of SDG outcomes, prompting a debate on the influence of data scarcity on countries' performance assessments. Ultimately, the absence of data, particularly high-quality data, jeopardises the success of sustainable development initiatives. The selection of well-defined and unambiguous indicators is paramount for each country to assess its current situation, develop actionable pathways for achieving objectives, and monitor progress effectively.

The sluggish progress observed in the implementation of the Sustainable Development Goals (SDGs) presents a glaring contrast with the potential consequences of failing to attain these objectives. The repercussions of falling short in achieving the SDGs are extensive and multifaceted. For instance, the attainment of the poverty reduction target holds paramount importance for every nation. Even under the most sanguine projections, several African countries, including Nigeria, Benin, Burundi, the Central African Republic, Malawi, Mali, Mozambique, Somalia, South Sudan, and Zambia, may face an additional 20% surge in poverty levels by 2030. These nations are also particularly susceptible to various climate-related hazards and disasters (Gertz and Kharas, 2018).

Moreover, economic development is intricately tied to education, a critical conduit for imparting the knowledge and skills requisite for the future of children and young adults. Unfortunately, the quality of education available to children often falls short of the required standards. In low-income countries, only 20% of children aged 3 to 6 have access to preschool education, while worldwide, the figure is as high as 50% (Leal Filho et al., 2020). Consequently, the absence of sustainable growth and environmental protection strategies may usher in significant challenges for future societies. Rapid and unsustainable economic growth could undermine the capacity of global systems to adapt to human well-being, thereby magnifying its impact on the environment (Leal Filho et al., 2020).

According to van Vuuren et al. (2022), the attainment of Sustainable Development Goals necessitates a profound transformation of contemporary societies, although defining the precise nature of this transformation remains a challenging endeavour. While there is a body of literature addressing strategies to achieve specific goals (e.g., climate action,

SDG13), there is a notable dearth of such guidance for many other objectives. Furthermore, there is a glaring scarcity of information regarding the simultaneous achievement of all SDGs. For instance, ensuring global food security (SDG2) may entail increased production, potentially resulting in heightened fertiliser use and consequent nitrous oxide emissions (SDG13) or exacerbating water scarcity issues (SDG6). Similarly, the pursuit of bioenergy to reduce greenhouse gas emissions (SDG13) may lead to an expansion of agricultural land, potentially reducing biodiversity. Nonetheless, there exist numerous synergies as well, such as the reduction of greenhouse gas emissions through the development of renewable energy (SDG13), which simultaneously curtails air pollutant emissions, thereby enhancing public health (SDG3).

To date, research efforts have predominantly focused on the individual implementation of specific Sustainable Development Goals at the national level or particular groupings of these goals. However, a conspicuous gap in the existing literature pertains to comprehensive analyses and scenarios aimed at achieving all 17 SDGs simultaneously. Various policy reports and scientific initiatives, including the Science-Based Goals Initiative and the UN Global Sustainability Report, have also underscored this knowledge deficiency.

Any endeavour geared toward conducting a quantitative analysis of the pathways to achieve the SDGs necessitates a precise delineation of the target space. This involves formulating a delimited set of objectives that are unambiguously expressed while offering comprehensive coverage of the SDGs' aspirations. The current framework, comprising 169 targets and 232 indicators for tracking progress towards the 2030 Agenda, is characterised by its overarching breadth, lack of structure, and intricate complexity. Moreover, these indicators may not consistently exhibit a robust scientific basis, further complicating their utility in supporting quantitative assessments of transition trajectories (van Vuuren et al., 2022). As a result, progress in developing scenarios at all regional levels (global, national, local) is hampered by the lack of a target area that could help the scientific community analyse the pathways to achieving the SDGs.

The formulation of the target space is being handled by experts participating in the "The World in 2050" (TWI2050, 2018) initiative. TWI2050's primary mission is to provide knowledge that can facilitate the political process and the effective implementation of the Sustainable Development Goals. This initiative operates through a voluntary and collaborative approach, engaging over 60 authors representing approximately 20 institutions and benefiting from the insights of around 100 independent experts hailing from academia, business, government, intergovernmental bodies, and non-governmental organisations across the globe. Together, they create scenarios for sustainable development pathways. The work by TWI2050 (2018) delineated six pivotal transformations that can pave the way for attaining the Sustainable Development Goals and ensuring long-term sustainable development by 2050 and beyond. These transformative areas encompass human potential and demography, consumption and production, decarbonisation and energy, food, biosphere and water, smart cities and the digital revolution. The report presents guiding principles and recommendations for orchestrating the integrated pathways essential for realising these transformations. Each transformation highlights the need for prioritised investments and regulatory actions, necessitating collaborative efforts between specific governmental bodies, businesses, and civil society. Consequently, these transformations can be orchestrated within the framework of governmental structures while duly acknowledging the intricate interconnections among the 17 SDGs.

The realisation of the Sustainable Development Goals exhibits notable variations across countries, primarily influenced by diverse factors encompassing social, economic, environmental, political, and institutional dimensions. Nonetheless, it is crucial to emphasise that the extent of this variability predominantly stems from the actions undertaken by governments aimed at concurrently advancing two or more SDGs. Consequently, an urgent imperative arises for research that delves into how countries perceive and prioritise the Sustainable Development Goals. Gaining a comprehensive understanding of the degree to which these objectives are attained and the intricate interdependencies among them is pivotal in formulating effective policies and allocating resources more strategically to facilitate their successful implementation.

The considerations delineated in this section underscore the multifaceted endeavours necessary for SDG achievement. These will include educating policymakers and society on sustainability, mobilising science to diagnose challenges, developing long-term pathways and tracking progress, and mobilising governments, businesses, and civil society.

REFERENCES

Akuraju, V., Pradhan, P., Haase, D., Kropp, J.P., Rybski, D. 2020. Relating SDG11 indicators and urban scaling – An exploratory study. *Sustainable Cities and Society*, 52, 101853, https://doi.org/10.1016/j.scs.2019.101853.

Alaimo, L.S., Ciacci, A., Ivaldi, E. 2021. Measuring Sustainable Development by Non-aggregative Approach. *Social Indicators Research*, 157, 101–122, https://doi.org/10.1007/s11205-020-02357-0.

Allen, C., Metternicht, G., Wiedmann, T. 2016. National Pathways to the Sustainable Development Goals (SDGs): A Comparative Review of Scenario Modelling Tools. *Environ Sci & Policy*, 66, 199–207, doi:10.1016/j.envsci.2016.09.008.

Bąk, I., Cheba, K. 2018. Study of spatial uniformity of sustainable development of the European Union before, during and after the economic crisis. *Przegląd Statystyczny. Statistical Review*, 65(2), 224–248, DOI 10.5604/01.3001.0014.0537.

Bąk, I., Cheba., K. 2020. Zielona gospodarka jako narzędzie zrównoważonego rozwoju. Wydawnictwo Uczelniane Zachodniopomorskiego Uniwersytetu Technologicznego w Szczecinie, Szczecin.

Berger, G., Zwirner, W. 2008. The Interfaces Between the EU SDS and the Lisbon Strategy: Objectives, Governance Provisions, Cooperative and Future Developments. ESDN Quarterly Report December 2008.

Brelsford, C., Lobo, J., Hand, J., & Bettencourt, L. M. A. 2017. Heterogeneity and scale of sustainable development in cities. *Proceedings of the National Academy of Sciences of the United States of America*, 114(34), 8963–8968. https://doi.org/10.1073/pnas.1606033114.

Büyüközkana, G., Karabulut, Y. 2018. Sustainability performance evaluation: Literature review and future directions. *J Environ Manage*, 217, 253–267. 10.1016/j.jenvman.2018.03.064

Carson R. 1962. *Silent Spring*. Houghton Mifflin Company.

Coopman, A., Osborn, D., Ullah, F., Auckland, E., Long, G. 2016. Seeing the whole. Implementing the SDGs in an Integrated and Coherent Way. Stakeholder forum, bioregional and Newcastle University.

Dobrzańska B.M. 2007. Planowanie strategiczne zrównoważonego rozwoju obszarów przyrodniczo cennych, Wydawnictwo Uniwersytetu w Białymstoku, Białystok.

Dos Santos, P.H., Neves, S.M., Sant'Anna, D,O., de Oliveira, C.H., Carvalho, H.D. 2019. The analytic hierarchy process supporting decision making for sustainable development: an overview of applications. *Journal of Clenear Production*, 212, 119–138, DOI: 10.1016/j.jclepro.2018.11.270.

Du Pisani J.A. 2006. Sustainable Development – historical roots of the concept. *Environmental sciences*, 3(2), 86–96.

Duran, D.C., Artene, A., Gogan, L.M., Duran, V. 2015. The Objectives of Sustainable Development – Ways to Achieve Welfare. *Procedia Economics and Finance*, 26, 812–817, https://doi.org/10.1016/S2212-5671(15)00852-7.

Egbende, L., Helldén, D., Mbunga, B., Schedwin, M., Kazenza, B., Viberg, N., Wanyenze, R., Ali, M.M., Alfvén, T. 2023. Interactions between Health and the Sustainable Development Goals: The Case of the Democratic Republic of Congo. *Sustainability*, 15, 1259, https://doi.org/10.3390/su15021259.

European Union. 2023. Sustainable development in the European Union Monitoring report on progress towards the SDGs in an EU context 2023 edition. Luxembourg: Publications Office of the European Union.

Eurostat. 2015. Sustainable development in the European Union 2015 monitoring report of the EU Sustainable Development Strategy. Luxembourg: Eurostat Statistical Books, Luxembourg.

Fader, M., Cranmer, C., Lawford, R., Engel-Cox, J. 2018. Toward an Understanding of Synergies and Trade-Offs Between Water, Energy, and Food SDG Targets. *Frontiers in Environmental Science*, 6, https://doi.org/10.3389/fenvs.2018.00112.

Fraisl, D., See, L., Sturn, T., MacFeely, S., Bowser, A., Campbell, J., Moorthy, I., Danylo, O., et al. 2022. Demonstrating the potential of Picture Pile as a citizen science tool for SDG monitoring. *Environmental Science & Policy*, 128, 81–93, 10.1016/j.envsci.2021.10.034.

Gertz, G., Kharas, H. 2018. Leave no country behind: ending poverty in the toughest places. Global Economy and Development Working Paper 110. Washington DC: Brookings Institution.

Griggs, D., Stafford-Smith, M., Gaffney, O. et al. 2013. Sustainable development goals for people and planet. *Nature*, 495, 305–307, https://doi.org/10.1038/495305a.

Golding, N., Burstein, R., Longbottom, J., Browne, A. J., Fullman, N., Osgood-Zimmerman, A., et al. 2017. Mapping under-5 and neonatal mortality in Africa, 2000–15: A baseline analysis for the sustainable development goals. *The Lancet*, 390(10108), 2171–2182. https://doi.org/10.1016/S0140-6736(17)31758-0.

Hellden, D., Weitz, N., Nilsson, M., Alfven, T. 2022. Situating Health Within the 2030 Agenda—A Practical Application of the Sustainable Development Goals Synergies Approach. *Public Health Reviews*, https://doi.org/10.3389/phrs.2022.1604350.

Horton, R. 2014. Offline: why the sustainable development goals will fail. *The Lancet*. 383(9936), 2196.

Huang, I.B, Keisler, J., Linkov, I. 2011. Multi-criteria decision analysis in environmental sciences: ten years of applications and trends. *Science of The Total Environment*, 409(19), 3578–3594, https://doi.org/10.1016/j.scitotenv.2011.06.022.

Kameyama, Y. 2004. Evaluation and Future of the Kyoto Protocol: Japan's Perspective. *International Review for Environmental Strategies*, 5(1), 71–82.

Kumar, S., Kumar, N., Vivekadhish, S. 2016. Millennium Development Goals (MDGs) to Sustainable Development Goals (SDGs): Addressing Unfinished Agenda and Strengthening Sustainable Development and Partnership. *Indian Journal of Community Medicine*, 41(1), 1–4. doi: 10.4103/0970-0218.170955. PMID: 26917865; PMCID: PMC4746946.

Leal Filho, W., Wolf, F., Lange Salvia, A. et al. 2020. Heading towards an unsustainable world: some of the implications of not achieving the SDGs. *Discover Sustainability*, 1(2), https://doi.org/10.1007/s43621-020-00002-x.

Maggino, F. 2017. Developing indicators and managing the complexity. In F. Maggino (Ed.), *Complexity in society: From indicators construction to their synthesis*. Cham, Springer, 87–114.

McArthur, J.W. 2014. The Origins of the Millennium Development Goals. *The SAIS Review of International Affairs*, 34(2), 5–24.

Meadows D. H., Meadows D. L., Randers J., Behrens III W. W. 1972. *The Limits to Growth: A report for the Club of Rome's project on the predicament of mankind*. A Potomac Associates Book.

Mitcham. C. 1995. The concept of sustainable development: its origins and ambivalence. *Technology in Society*, 17(3), 311–326, DOI: 10.1016/0160-791X(95)00008-F.

Moyer, J., Bohl, D. 2019. Alternative pathways to human development: assessing trade-offs and synergies in achieving the Sustainable Development Goals. *Futures* 105: 199–210, DOI:10.1016/j.futures.2018.10.007.

Moyer, J., Hedden, S. 2020. Are we on the right path to achieve the sustainable development goals? *World Development*, 127, 104749, https://doi.org/10.1016/j.worlddev.2019.104749.

Munda, G. 2008. The issue of consistency: basic discrete multi-criteria "Methods". Social multi-criteria evaluation for a sustainable economy. Springer, Berlin, 85–109.

Nerini, F., Tomei, J., Bisaga, I., Parikh, P., Czarny, M., Borrion, A., Spataru, C., Broto, V.C., Anandaradża, G., Milligana, B., Mulugetta, J. 2018. Mapping synergies and trade-offs between energy and the sustainable development goals. *Nature Energy*, 3, 10–15.

Nilashi, M., Boona, O.K., Wei-Han Tan, G., Lin, B., Abumalloh, R.A. 2023. Critical Data Challenges in Measuring the Performance of Sustainable Development Goals: Solutions and the Role of Big Data Analytics. *HDSR*, Issue 5.3, Summer. DOI: 10.1162/99608f92.545db2cf.

Noga, J., Wolbringa, G. 2013. An Analysis of the United Nations Conference on Sustainable Development (Rio +20) Discourse Using an Ability Expectation Lens. *Sustainability*, 5(9), 3615–3639, https://doi.org/10.3390/su5093615.

Nunes, A.R., Lee, K., O'Riordan, T. 2016. The importance of an integrating framework for achieving the Sustainable Development Goals: the example of health and well-being. *BMJ Global Health*, 1, e000068, doi:10.1136/bmjgh-2016-000068.

Omer, M.A.B., Noguchi, T. 2020. A conceptual framework for understanding the contribution of building materials in the achievement of Sustainable Development Goals (SDGs). *Sustainable Cities and Society*, 52, https://doi.org/10.1016/j.scs.2019.101869.

Osborn, D., Cutter, A., Ullah, F. 2015. Universal Sustainable Development Goals. Understanding the Transformational Challenge for Developed Countries. Report Of A Study By Stakeholder Forum, https://sustainabledevelopment.un.org/content/documents/1684SF_-_SDG_Universality_Report_-_May_2015.pdf.

Pham-Truffert, M., Metz, F., Fischer, M., Rueff, H., Masserli, P. 2020. Interactions among Sustainable Development Goals: Knowledge for identifying multipliers and virtuous cycles. *Sustainable Development*, 28(5), 1236–1250, https://doi.org/10.1002/sd.2073.

Pradhan, P., Costa, L., Rybski, D., Lucht, W., & Kropp, J. P. (2017). A systematic study of sustainable development goal (SDG) interactions. *Earth's Future*, 5(11), 1169–1179. https://doi.org/10.1002/2017EF000632.

Rocha,N.P., Dias, A., Santinha, G., Rodrigues, M., Queirós, A., Rodrigues, C. (2019). Smart Cities and Public Health: A Systematic Review. *Procedia Computer Science*, 164, 516–523. https://doi.org/10.1016/j.procs.2019.12.214.

Roszkowska, E., Filipowicz-Chomko, M. 2020. Measuring sustainable development in the education area using multi-criteria methods: a case study. *Central European Journal of Operations Research*, 28, 1219–1241, https://doi.org/10.1007/s10100-019-00641-0.

Scherer, L., Behrens, P., de Koning, A., Heijungs, R., Sprecher, B., Tukker, A. 2018. Trade-offs between social and environmental Sustainable Development Goals. *Environmental Science and Policy*, 90, 65–72, https://doi.org/10.1016/j.envsci.2018.10.002.

Schmidt-Trauba, G., Kroll, C., Teksoz, K., Durand-Delacre, D., Sachs, J. D. 2017. National baselines for the sustainable development goals assessed in the SDG index and dashboards. *Nature Geoscience*, 10, 547–555, https://doi.org/10.1038/ngeo2985.

Sompolska-Rzechuła, A., Kurdyś-Kujawska, A., 2021. Towards understanding interactions between sustainable development goals: the role of climate-wellbeing linkages. Experiences of EU countries. *Energies* 14 (7), 2025. https://doi.org/ 10.3390/en14072025.

Stafford-Smith, M., Griggs, D, Gaffney, O, Ullah, F, Reyers, B, Kanie, N, Stigson, B, Shrivastava, P, Leach, M, O'Connell, D. 2017. Integration: the key to implementing the Sustainable Development Goals. *Sustain Sci.* 2017;12(6): 911–919. doi: 10.1007/s11625-016-0383-3. Epub 2016 Jul 18. PMID: 30147763; PMCID: PMC6086249.

Tu, Y. 2018. Urban debates for climate change after the Kyoto Protocol. *Urban Studies*, 55(1), 3–18. https://doi.org/10.1177/0042098017717363.

Ture, H., Dogan, S., Kocak, D. 2019. Assessing euro 2020 strategy using multicriteria decision making methods: VIKOR and TOPSIS. *Social Indicators Research*, 142(2), 645–665, DOI: 10.1007/s11205-018-1938-8.

TWI2050. 2018. The World in 2050. Transformations to Achieve the Sustainable Development Goals. Report Prepared by the World in 2050 Initiative (International Institute for Applied Systems Analysis (IIASA)).

United Nations. 2015. Transforming our world: the 2030 Agenda for Sustainable Development. Resolution adopted by the General Assembly on 25 September 2015, A/RES/70/1.

van Vuuren,D.P., Zimm, C., Busch, S., Kriegler E., Leininger, J., Messner, D., Nakicenovic,N., Rockstrom, J., Riahi, K., Sperling, F., Bosetti, V., Cornell, S., Gaffney, O.,Lucas, P.L., Popp, A., Ruhe, C., von Schiller, A., Schmidt, J.O., Soergel, B. (2022). Defining a sustainable development target space for 2030 and 2050. *One Earth*, 5(2). 142-156, https://doi.org/10.1016/j.oneear.2022.01.003.

Wang, M., Janssen, A.B.G., Bazin, J., Strokal, M., Mia, L., Kroeze, C. 2022. Accounting for interactions between Sustainable Development Goals is essential for water pollution control in China. *Nature Communications*, 13(730).

Warchold, A., Pradhana, P., Kroppa, J.P. 2020. Variations in sustainable development goal interactions: Population, regional, and income disaggregation. *Sustainable Development*, https://doi.org/10.1002/sd.2145.

WCED (World Commission on Environment and Development). 1987. Our common future. Oxford: Oxford University Press.

Yang, S., Zhao, W., Liu, Y., Cherubini, F., Fu, B., Pereira, P., 2020. Prioritizing sustainable development goals and linking them to ecosystem services: a global expert's knowledge evaluation. *Geogr. Sustain.* 1 (4), 321–330. https://doi.org/10.1016/j. geosus.2020.09.004.

Zinatizadeh, S., Azimi, A., Monavari, S.M., Sobhanardakani, S. 2017. Multi-criteria decision making for sustainability evaluation in urban areas: a case study for Kermanshah city, Iran. *Applied Ecology and Environmental Research*, 15(4),1083–1100, DOI: http://dx.doi.org/10.15666/aeer/1504 _10831100.

3. Financial markets toward sustainability and Environmental, Social, Governance (ESG) risk: Sustainable Development Goals (SDGs) context

Magdalena Ziolo

3.1 SUSTAINABILITY IMPACT ON FINANCIAL MARKETS

The concept of sustainability first appeared during considerations and discussions initiated by the expansive development of agriculture and the associated high consumption of wood, which resulted in deforestation and, consequently, limited nutritional resources for farm animals and people. It led to famines, epidemics, and population depopulation in Europe in the 14th century. In the 17th century, Hans Carl von Carlowitz, in his work *Sylvicultura Oeconomica*, referred to the concept of sustainability understood as "not using more resources than can be regenerated during the same period" and became the precursor of the described idea (Vogt and Weber, 2019, p. 1). References to sustainability can also be found in the works of A. Smith, who pointed out that capitalist systems must be based on honesty and coherence to function correctly in the long term. Otherwise, they will be destroyed (Niemczyk, 2017, p. 12). Sustainability is treated as good management, future-oriented, responsible, and for a common future (Vogt and Weber, 2019, p. 1). "Common future" is also the title of the Brundtland Report (1987), which contains one of the most frequently used definitions of sustainable development, stating that it is the development that "ensures that the needs of present generations are met without compromising the ability to meet the needs of future generations" (WCED, 1987). In 1992, the United

Nations Conference on the Environment and Development (UNCED) (Earth Summit) was held in Rio de Janeiro, during which it was agreed that sustainable development should be in the center of attention of the global community. The Earth Summit included The Rio Declaration on Environment and Development (RD). Then, in 2000, the so-called Millennium Development Goals were established at the UN Millennium Summit. The Goals (Goal 7) included maintaining and supporting environmental sustainability. The Millennium Development Goals, like the definitions of sustainable development, have evolved. Currently, they are Sustainable Development Goals (17 SDGs under Agenda 21). A significant trend in the evolution of the approach to understanding sustainable development and its goals was expanding the definitional scope to many areas, including the financial sphere. Sustainable development requires financing (Crona et al., 2021). Conventional finance is unsuitable for financing sustainable development due to the complexity of sustainable development and the challenges and requirements related to providing financing for this type of development process. It is expressed in particular through the approach to the role and function of finance, the categories of profit and risk, and the approach to the perception of value and economic benefit. In this context, several questions arise about methods, instruments, and forms of funding against the background of factors that strongly differentiate sustainable development and financial institutions. It should be noted that Pisano et al., in 2012, pointed out the need to adapt the financial sector to the requirements of sustainable development, justifying their approach with limitations on the financial industry (Table 3.1).

Since 2012, when Pisano et al. proposed the comparison of the financial sector and sustainable development, the financial industry and finance have evolved significantly towards the sustainable finance paradigm. Kumar et al. (2022) discussed the definition and concept of sustainable finance comprehensively. They deemed the EC (European Commission) definition of sustainable finance, that defines sustainable finance as "an evolving process of considering environmental, social, and governance (ESG) factors in financial and investment decisions," as too narrow (EC, 2021). There are many definitions of sustainable finance, and no unified approach exists. The broader and the most general definition of sustainable finance refers to the sustainability context (Kumar et al. 2022). Following the report proposed by Kumar et al. (2022), "sustainable finance should encompass all activities and factors that would make finance sustainable and contribute to sustainability." This understanding

Table 3.1   Sustainable development and the financial sector

Sustainable Development	Financial Sector
Three-dimensional approach: finding a balance between: environmental sustainability, social sustainability, and economic development Long-term horizon and intergenerational equity; Protecting the natural environment, imposing restrictions on economic growth; Equal opportunities, accessibility, mitigating income disparities; Social inclusion and participation; Governance, good governance.	A one-dimensional approach toward maximizing profits and return on investment; Short-term perspective, discounting, calculations based on Present Value; Low or no awareness of the impact of financial decisions on the environment; Limited understanding of the results of financial decisions and their consequences for society; High complexity, no inclusion; Efficiency orientation, lack of transparency.

Source: Own elaboration based on: U. Pisano, A. Martinuzzi, and B. Bruckner, *The Financial Sector and Sustainable Development: Logics, principles and actors,* ESDN Quarterly Report N°27, December 2012, p. 27.

of sustainable finance covers all stakeholders' perspectives and goals. Based on research published, sustainability impacts financial markets in many ways; one is the impact on financial performance (Rahi et al., 2022). Nizam et al. (2019) diagnose the channels through which environmental and social sustainability performance positively affect a bank's financial performance. Sustainability affects the financial sector directly and indirectly. According to Regulation (EU) 2019/2088 of The European Parliament and of The Council of 27 November 2019 on sustainability-related disclosures in the financial services sector, sustainability risk means "an environmental, social or governance event or condition that, if it occurs, could cause a negative material impact on the value of the investment (...)". The direct impact of sustainability on financial institutions is expressed through the so-called physical risk. It concerns the possibility of loss or destruction of fixed assets, e.g., due to climate change (e.g., floods resulting in flooding of buildings). In turn, the indirect impact of the so-called transition risk affects the financial sector, indirectly influencing the items that shape the financial result. Sources of physical and transition risks are presented in Table 3.2.

The IMF (2022) points out that sustainability impacts financial stability through multiple channels: environmental risk exposures, governance

Table 3.2   Sources of physical and transition risks

Physical risk	Transition risk
Extreme weather events	Changing public policies
Ecosystem pollution	Technological changes
Raising water levels	Changes in behavior and
Water shortage	mood
Deforestation/desertification	New business models

Source: Overview of Environmental Risk Analysis by Financial Institutions.
Network for Greening the Financial System Technical Document, Central Banks
and Supervisors, September 2020, p. 5.

failures, and social risks. Environmental risks, especially climate-related
risks, may lead to financial losses, bankruptcy, or financial distress of
financial companies due to the impact of natural disasters. Climate
change may cause financial institutions, asset owners, and firms losses.
Governance risks were observed during the 2008 financial crisis that
caused significant losses for the financial industry, and as a result, public
aid for financial institutions was a must. Social risks like, among other
things, inequalities, financial exclusion, and an aging society can also
be a reason for financial instability because of the impact on demand for
financial products and services (IMF, 2022). Nowadays, financial sectors must be stable, safe, and sustainable. However, there is a risk that
the financial sector will not implement sustainability practices because
it "follows a logic that contradicts the purely economic rationale" (Rahi
et al., 2022). Mitigating sustainability risk requires instruments and a
legal and organizational framework, so the new, sustainable finance
paradigm evolved (Sun et al., 2011). Financial markets are transforming,
stimulated by the impact of sustainability. Financial institutions operating within financial markets, considering the effect of sustainability risk
on their activities, undertake several actions to reduce the impact of this
risk. These activities result, on the one hand, from applicable regulations
and legal conditions and, on the other hand, from initiatives undertaken
by financial institutions themselves (Table 3.3).

Initiatives (Table 3.3) to ensure and develop sustainable finance on
financial markets are two-track and result from legal provisions adopted
at the level of the European Union and individual countries (including
member states) as well as internal regulations and initiatives of financial
institutions. These activities are expressed, among others, in initiatives

Table 3.3   Initiatives of the financial sector towards sustainability

Sector/Scope	Initiatives
Banking	UN Principles for Responsible Banking; Principles for Positive Impact Finance; Equator Principles; Green Loan Principles; Green Bond Principles; Social Bond Principles; Sustainability Bond Principles; Task Force on Climate Related Disclosures; Global Reporting Initiative; Sustainability Reporting Guidelines; Framework for Reporting Environmental Information; Sustainability Accounting Tools; European Commission Action Plan; Global Alliance for Banking on Values; Climate Stress Tests; Banking Environment Initiative; The Network of Central Banks and Supervisors for Greening the Financial System
Insurance	Principles for Sustainable Insurance; Equator Principles; Task Force on Climate Related Disclosures; Global Reporting Initiative; Sustainability Reporting Guidelines; Framework for Reporting Environmental Information; European Commission Action Plan
Asset management	Principles for Responsible Investment; Sustainable Blue Economy Finance Principles; Principles for Positive Impact Finance; Equator Principles; Green Loan Principles; Green Bond Principles; Social Bond Principles; Climate Bonds Initiative; Sustainability Bond Principles; Task Force on Climate Related Disclosures; Global Reporting Initiative; Sustainability Reporting Guidelines; Framework for Reporting Environmental Information; Sustainability Accounting Tools; European Commission Action Plan;
Investment funds	Global Reporting Initiative; Sustainability Reporting Guidelines; Framework for Reporting Environmental Information; European Commission Action Plan; Occupational Retirement Provision Directive
Capital market	Sustainable Stock Exchanges Initiative; Global Reporting Initiative; Sustainability Reporting Guidelines; Framework for Reporting Environmental Information; European Commission Action Plan

Sector/Scope	Initiatives
Common initiatives	United Nations Environment Program Finance Initiative – UNEPFI; ISO 14001; ISO26000; Global Reporting Initiative; Recommendations from the UNEP Finance Initiatives (FI) Rio Roundtable; The Collevecchio Declaration on Financial Institutions and Sustainability; Declaration on Climate Change by the Financial Services Sector; Carbon Principles; Sustainable Finance Disclosure Regulation – SFDR; The Portfolio Decarbonization Coalition; Global Partnership for Financial Inclusion; The Investment Leaders Group; Climatewise; The 1-in-100 Initiative; Global Impact Investing Network

Source: Own elaboration based on: M. Ziolo, Financial markets and climate change. Dilemmas and challenges versus sustainable development goals, *Studia BAS*, 2(74)2023, p. 24; www.sia-partners.com/en/news-and-publications/from -our-experts/changing-dynamics-sustainable-finance-regulatory-push (Accessed: 6.10.2023).

of international organizations associating with financial institutions or global enterprises in the field of ESG regarding financial markets, activities of central banks, good practices and industry codes, and activities undertaken at individual financial institutions. Aspinall et al. (2015) attempted to organize a rich body of work focused on finding the relationship between financial systems and "sustainability" (Aspinall et al., 2018, pp. 1–21). They reviewed 355,000 articles published in 125 selected journals and indicated, among others, the study of Goldstein (2001), who concludes, based on the experience of Costa Rica, that financial markets and financial institutions, giant banks, are a factor limiting sustainable development. One of the reasons for this state of affairs is that financial institutions prefer to finance long-term consumption and the real estate market. Therefore, there is low interest on the part of both banks and capital markets in funding the so-called "green" technologies and "green" consumerism. At the same time, Goldstein points to the need for reforms that would create incentives for financing projects that reduce the impact of adverse external effects. An essential role in this respect concerns regulatory policy regarding green banking products and green financial markets (mainly bonds) (Goldstein, 2001, pp. 199–215). Huang (2012) observed that production, as an effect of economic activity, affects the volume of natural resources, which depletes as production increases, and thus, production variability harms the level of savings (Aspinall et al., 2018, p. 13).

3.2 ESG RISK AND FINANCIAL MARKETS

ESG (Environmental, social, governance) is gaining importance, mainly because of ESG risk and the development of ESG reporting. Non-financial reporting is crucial because it shows the various threats and the possibilities of overcoming them (including in the context of taxation). Ensuring the availability of independent, prestigious audit services is, in turn, a prerequisite for high-quality internal control and risk control (S&P Global Ratings, 2018). ESG risks have been defined by the European Banking Authority (EBA) as "the risks of any negative financial impact on the institution stemming from the current or prospective impacts of ESG factors on its counterparties or invested assets." ESG risk consists of environmental risk, social risk, and governance risk. Among the factors determining environmental risk, the most commonly mentioned are climate change, environmental pollution (air, water, land), degradation of the natural environment, and resource scarcity (Escrig-Olmedo, Fernández-Izquierdo, Ferre-ro-Ferrero, Rivera-Lirio and Muñoz-Torres, 2019). Environmental risk may affect the creditworthiness and liquidity of a company. The second category included in ESG is social risk, defined as the broadest category and the one with the fastest development potential. The risk factors include consumer rights, health risks, human rights, employee rights, safety risks, strikes, and protests. The factors impacting the level of governance risk include governance, business ethics, risk management, crisis management, respect for the rights of stakeholders, prevention of corruption, transparency, and the method of remunerating management board members. When analyzing an organization in terms of management risk, attention is paid to the following factors: effectiveness, stability, predictability of policies and operating strategies, institutional (including social) responsibility, and transparency, which have a direct impact on creditworthiness. The growing importance of ESG factors in risk valuation affects financial phenomena, processes, and assessment methods. The literature raises two overarching issues related to research on non-financial factors (Friede et al., 2003, pp. 210–230, Schmidt and Rynes, 2003, pp. 403–411):

• the impact of ESG factors on the financial standing (Delmas and Blass, 2010, pp. 245–260) and,

- ways of incorporating ESG factors into the decision-making processes of financial institutions (Friede et al., 2015, pp. 1–27).

Referring to these two streams of research, it is worth pointing out the definitional context of ESG. UNEP FI indicates that this term should be understood as environmental, social, and corporate governance issues that investors consider in the context of corporate behavior. The list of factors creating ESG is not fixed or closed; in the general approach to ESG, it is noted that these are (UNEP FI, 2019):

- non-financial, intangible factors;
- phenomena considered in the medium or long term;
- factors that have no monetary dimension;
- externalities;
- changing regulations and public policy frameworks;
- specific patterns resulting from the supply chain;
- issues of public concern.

Based on the literature review, the development of the concept of Corporate Social Responsibility (CSR) is responsible for the emergence of a new category of risk referred to as ESG and understood as "the potential impact of stakeholders on the enterprise" or, conversely, "the risk to which the enterprise exposes its stakeholders when conducting business activities" (ORSE, 2012). According to another approach, ESG is a new dimension of Socially Responsible Investing (SRI) (Rice et al., 2012). At the same time, attention is drawn to the fact that ESG is a risk of an external nature, which is not determined by the financing structure and may affect the financial condition of the entity and its assets. In addition to the financial problems that ESG risk may evaluate, it may also threaten asset holders and business partners (Inderst, 2011). ESG is functioning near sustainability; however, ESG is instead a term popular among investors, and companies prefer sustainability. The term "ESG," which refers to a group of non-financial factors, has been used since 2004. Then, as part of the UN Global Compact's "Who Cares Wins" initiative, attention was drawn to the connections and dependencies between environmental, social, and management factors (Stampe, 2014, p. 12). These factors are strongly related to sustainable development.

As Scholtens (2006) points out, finances are an essential determinant of sustainable development, hence the frequent analysis of the relationships between financial and non-financial factors (Scholtens, 2006, pp. 19–33). The research results emphasize the link between the financial results or, more broadly, the financial standing of enterprises and ESG factors. Orlitzky et al. (2003) showed a positive correlation between social and environmental factors and the economic crisis (Scholtens, 2006, pp. 19–33). A study conducted by Velte (2017) on a group of 80 companies also confirmed the existence of such relationships, particularly the impact of ESG factors on ROA (Velte, 2017, pp. 169–178). Friede et al. (2015), analyzing research results presented in over 2,000 scientific articles, confirmed the dominant, positive impact of ESG factors on the financial situation (Friede et al., 2015, pp. 210–233). The importance of ESG risk has increased in the public discussion and regulatory proposals that appeared after the 2008 crisis, including The Europe 2020 document, which contains references and recommendations regarding ESG in the context of SRI and the need to repair the financial system after the 2008 crisis by changing the way of thinking about finance and financial markets. This change is expressed primarily in the emphasis on the social context of finance and the responsibility of financial markets towards society for financial decisions. Keefe (2011) and Viederman (2009) draw attention to the role of ESG factors in the context of their importance for financial institutions.

The authors raise the issue of the need to include ESG factors in financial institutions' procedures and decisions, thus ensuring more effective risk management. In 1992, the United Nations recommended incorporating ESG factors into financial decisions. Due to the growing threat of ESG risk, these recommendations are becoming more and more valid. Analysis of applicable documents such as Basel II, Basel III (standards for operational risk in banks; monitoring of environmental risk about legal repayment security); ISO26000 (reference to the concept of socially responsible business – CSR); and GRI and EFFAS indicators for monitoring the effectiveness of ESG risk management confirm that there are formal bases for further in-depth actions aimed at full integration of ESG risk in the decisions of financial institutions. ESG factors are also present in the methodologies of sustainable rating agencies (SRA). ESG risk affects banking risk, mainly through the impact of environmental risk on credit risk. Environmental risk affects the financial standing of enterprises that operate in "environmentally sensitive" sectors. These entities are obliged to comply with environmental protection regulations and adapt their activities in such a way as to meet environmental requirements. Banks cooperating with companies with high environmental risk exposure are also prone to reputation risk. The failure of the ability to generate income is also determined by health risk classified as social risk, which strongly affects the economy and the creditworthiness of business entities. This situation is noticed in the era of a pandemic (example: COVID-19) when the actions taken by governments radically influenced the basic macroeconomic parameters (GDP, inflation, unemployment, interest rates, deficit, and public debt) and the financial situation of monetary and non-monetary institutions.

3.3 THE ROLE OF FINANCIAL MARKETS IN ACHIEVING SDGS

In September 2015, 193 countries signed the so-called 2030 Agenda. The Agenda includes 17 SDGs (Sustainable Development Goals), and 169 targets and aims to ensure sustainable (and inclusive) growth and development. The SDGs are aimed at reducing negative externalities related to human activities through issues of social inclusion (SDGs 1–11, 15, 16), environmental protection (SDGs: 1, 2, 6–9, 11–15) and interdisciplinary actions (SDGs: 3, 4, 10–14, 16, 17). The Sustainable Development Goals are a strong stimulus determining activity toward sustainable development and growth (Ziolo et al., 2021). According to the United Nations Sustainable Development Group, USD 3.3–4.5 trillion per year must be spent to achieve the 2030 Agenda for Sustainable Development (UN Sustainable Development Group, 2023). The International Monetary Fund offers several initiatives supporting the financing of the SDGs at every single country level (IMF, 2023); it is essential in developing countries with an SDGs annual average funding gap of USD 2.5 trillion (UN Sustainable Development Group, 2023). The implementation of the SDGs is monitored at the level of the European Union member states (Europe Sustainable Development Report 2022). The SDGs are integrated into public policies (Lencucha et al., 2023), affecting the allocation and flow of financial capital. The implementation of the SDGs is not possible without the active participation of financial markets, which provide capital to finance activities, e.g., investments necessary to implement individual SDGs, but also meet the demand for financial products and services needed to implement the goals included in the SDGs. Based on related work, publications in the scope of relationships between finance and SDGs discuss mainly sources of financing – micro and macro level, public and private (Kharas et al., 2015); the financing mechanism (Sachs, 2015); SDG investing and sustainable finance (Zhan and Santos-Paulino; 2021); or challenges (Barua, 2020). Makarenko et al. (2018) identified the targets for each SDG and refer to the role of the financial sector in achieving a particular SDG (Table 3.4).

Table 3.4   SDGs and financial markets

Sustainable Development Goal	Target	Activity of financial markets in achieving SDGs
SDG1 No poverty	Target 1.4	Providing financial resources and services; protecting the rights of consumers of financial services;
SDG5 Gender equality	Target 5.5	Delivering equal access to financial products and services and equal treatment of women and men, including remuneration and promotion policy;
SDG8 Decent work and economic growth	Target 8.1	Socially responsible investments; investment strategies including ESG
SDG10 Reduced inequalities	Target 10.5	Stability and safety of the financial sector, especially systemic risk, solvency, and responsibility of financial markets;
SDG12 Responsible consumption and production	Target 12.6	Building a benchmark market (comparability of indicators linked to sustainable development) and unified requirements for disclosure of information by companies, borrowers, and financial markets;
SDG13 Climate action	Target 13.1 Target 13.2	Environmental and social impact through financial products and services; support for sustainable development policies by financial markets; building new markets and demand for financial services and products ensuring SDGs; incorporating ESG in risk assessment, strategies and the decisions-making process;
SDG17 Partnership for the goals	Target 17.16	Cooperation networks and ensuring communication among stakeholders to achieve SDGs

Source: Own elaboration based on: Makarenko, Y. Yelnikova, A. Lasukova, A.R. Barhaq: *Corporate social responsibility of financial sector institutions in the light of sustainable development goals financing: the role of banks and stock exchanges.* Public and Municipal Finance 2018, 7(3), s. 1–14. doi:10.21511/pmf.07(3).2018.01; M. Ziolo, Financial markets and climate change. Dilemmas and challenges versus sustainable development goals, *Studia BAS*, 2(74) 2023, p. 24.

Financial markets comprehensively impact implementing the SDGs, reflected in direct and indirect actions. Immediate actions concern financing for implementing the SDGs or, more broadly, mobilizing capital for sustainable funding (Griffiths, 2018). However, the indirect impact on the implementation of the SDGs concerns activities such as 1/ mitigating ESG risk through risk management and transfer, 2/ providing sustainable financial services and products, 3/ transfer of knowledge and good practices, 4/ client policy, 5/ supporting SDGs by financial innovations. Weber (2018) identified financial products and services addressing SDGs (Table 3.5).

SDG5 and SDG13 have the most scope of interest in reporting and actions taken by financial institutions. In turn, goal 14 (Life below water), not included in Table 3.5, is rarely considered by financial markets.[1] Makarenko et al. (2018) identified some barriers to financing of SDGs by financial markets, including, among others:

- incorporating negative environmental externalities and ESG criteria in the investment decision-making process in the financial sector and business practice;
- new investment opportunities and their specificity in the strategies of financial institutions;
- new competencies, new types of financing for sustainable development and SDGs;
- information asymmetry among participants of the investment process;
- common standards for disclosing information and understanding ESG criteria;
- reorientation of financial instruments towards long-term financing.

Zhanand Santos-Paulino (2021) discuss the role of capital markets globally in covering the SDGs funding gap. The authors pointed out that the target of sustainability funds are mainly sectors such as clean energy, clean technology, sustainable agriculture, and food security. The authors assume that in the group of sustainability dedicated instruments are, among others – sustainability-themed funds, green bonds, and social bonds; and according to UNCTAT (2020), funds financing sustainable investment have reached $1.2–$1.3 trillion today (Zhan and Santos-Paulino, 2021). The authors also pointed out the role of stock exchanges and regulators. Stock exchanges are a kind of exchange platform for

Table 3.5   SDGs and related financial product and services

Sustainable Development Goal	Financial products and services
SDG1 No poverty	Private international development finance
SDG2 Zero hunger	Microfinance
SDG3 Good health and well-being	Health-care investments
SDG4 Quality of education	Donations
SDG5 Gender inequality	Microfinance and lending to women and female entrepreneurs
SDG6 Clean water and sanitation	Socially responsible mutual funds investing in water
SDG7 Affordable and clean energy	Renewable energy investment
SDG8 Decent work and economic growth	General investments into the real economy
SDG9 Industry innovation and infrastructure	Project finance and commercial lending integrating social and environmental criteria for lending decisions
SDG10 Reduced inequalities	Fair payment of financial sector employees
SDG11 Sustainable cities and communities	Mortgage lending
SDG12 Responsible consumption and production	Socially responsible investing
SDG13 Climate action	Climate finance
SDG14 Life below water	Blue financing
SDG15 Life on land	Financing sustainable services
SDG16 Peace, justice and strong institutions	Lending to public institutions

Source: Own elaboration based on: O. Weber, *The Financial Sector and the SDGs Interconnections and Future Directions,* CIGI Papers No. 201, Centre for International Governance and Innovation 2018, p. 7.

sustainable finance and a roadmap for corporate governance. SDGs, especially SDGs 1, 2, 8, 12, and 13, positively impact regulations and increase investor pressure. According to the review of GreenBiz (2023), financial services companies are willing to finance mainly SDG1 (no poverty), SDG5 (gender equality), SDG8 (decent work and economic growth), and SDG13 (climate action). At the same time, the financial institutions find it very difficult to navigate among the 169 targets the SDGs consist of.

3.4 CRITICAL REMARKS

The role of financial markets and institutions seems to be especially important for catching the green and blue wave as providers of credit and financial resources must decide where to invest and consider different risk factors and how to contribute to sustainable development through the core business (Scholtens, 2006). The changing European regulatory framework will foster the European financial market to mainstream environmental factors into risk management. The European Union is nowadays a leader in sustainable financing because of its regulations, policies, and strategies focused on climate change (especially the reduction in GHG emissions, for example, EU Taxonomy, Fit for 55, assets typology, and sustainable finance disclosure, among others). Providing innovative, sustainable green and blue financing requires the involvement of all stakeholders. To do so, they must be defined along with their role in the financing mechanism if, in particular, it concerns public sector entities (i.e., governments), the enterprise sector, or NGOs.

Financing the SDGs through financial markets faces many challenges and dilemmas. When discussing policy framework for financing sustainable development, Zhan and Santos-Paulino (2021) formulate recommendations to accelerate achieving SDGs through sustainable investment. The authors focus on the following issues:

- finding a balance between liberalization and regulation;
- finding a trade-off between the risk-return rates and accessible and affordable services for all;
- searching for a balance between a push for private investment and public investment;
- finding a balance between the global scope of the SDGs and the need to make a special effort in least-developed countries (LDCs) and other vulnerable economies;
- mainstreaming the SDGs in investment policies;
- creating SDG model zones;
- ESG standards, compliance, and reporting;
- incorporating SMEs in compliance and ESG reporting;
- sustainable development and family businesses.

The challenges identified by the authors relate to public and private financing and all stakeholders in financing the SDGs. When analyzing the challenges facing finance and financial markets in funding the SDGs, it is worth paying attention to the following critical points. Currently, the issues of concern include gaps in financing, the low diversity in financing with a high concentration of funds primarily for improving energy efficiency, the lack of a theoretical framework and definitions, financing opportunities based on conventional sources, non-bankable projects, and the lack of an established effective financial mechanism for the SDGs. Financial markets are subject to regulations, including regulations regarding ESG. Hence, the approach of markets and institutions differs in individual countries. The European Union is currently the most advanced when it comes to the standardization of ESG requirements and regulations. Hence, financial institutions, including the ECB and EBA, propose specific definitional and regulatory solutions and standards.

Financial markets and institutions face a dilemma related to customer segmentation and selecting a business model to minimize reputational risk. Many of the current clients of financial institutions are companies with high exposure to ESG risk, so the question arises of how further to shape the path of cooperation with dirty business companies and whether to continue such collaboration. From the point of view of financing the SDGs, all entities should be included in this process and provided with financing for projects with a positive impact on sustainability and the implementation of the SDGs.

Another issue is shaping the risk management systems of financial markets and institutions in terms of mitigating ESG risk and, consequently, incorporating ESG risk into financial decisions and risk management systems, including scoring systems. Many financial markets and institutions have already tried and implemented such procedures. However, these systems need more differentiation and incomparability and, therefore, different financing conditions offered by financial institutions to entities applying for such financing. Financial institutions and markets must also report ESG, and good practices in this area are still being developed. Solutions regarding reporting standards differ between countries and are incomparable. There is also a need for a global ESG database enabling comprehensive ESG risk management at markets and financial institutions worldwide.

Another significant issue concerns how to transition unsustainable behaviors and activities into sustainable counterparts. Often, projects rejected by institutions and financial markets as harmful to sustainability are financed from public funds due to the need to maintain jobs or the influence of the political lobby. The need for coherence in decision-making regarding financing by financial markets and institutions is a real challenge in implementing the SDGs.

Summarized considerations on the challenges facing the financial market in building a sustainable financial system at the global level include:

- development of methods for assessing financial systems based on ESG factors;
- development of a taxonomy of ESG risk-weighted assets;
- implementation of integrated reporting taking into account the impact of ESG factors on financial transactions and operations conducted by financial institutions;
- undertaking activities in the field of inter-sectoral and inter-institutional cooperation to ensure sustainable practices in the financial sector and between the public and financial sector;
- development of a global ESG risk map;
- monitoring of cash flows in the scope of sustainable finance;
- monitoring the greening and catching the blue waves of financial markets;
- assessing the effectiveness of sustainable financing;
- launching a mechanism for reporting by financial institutions on initiatives for sustainable development.

NOTE

1. https://capitalmonitor.ai/institution/banks/how-banks-are-reporting-on-the-sdgs/ (Accessed: 6.10.2023).

REFERENCES

Aspinall, N.G., Jones, S.R., McNeill, E.H. Werner, R.A & Zalk, T. (2018). Sustainability and the financial system, *British Actuarial Journal, 23*, 1–21.

Barua, S. (2020). Financing sustainable development goals: A review of challenges and mitigation strategies. *Business Strategy & Development*, 3(3), 277–293

BlackRock and Ceres (2015). "21st Century Engagement: Investor Strategies for Incorporating ESG Considerations into Corporate Interactions"; "About Us," Ceres, https://www.ceres.org/about-us (Accessed 22.03.2023)

Chakroun, S., Salhi, B., Ben Amar, A. and Jarboui, A. (2020). The impact of ISO 26000 social responsibility standard adoption on firm financial performance:

Evidence from France, *Management Research Review*, *43*(5), 545–571. https://doi.org/10.1108/MRR-02-2019-0054

Crona B., Eriksson K., Lerpold K., Malmström M., Sanctuary M., Sandberg J. (2021). Transforming toward sustainability through financial markets: Four challenges and how to turn them into opportunities, *One Earth*, Volume 4, Issue 5, Pages 599–601, ISSN 2590-3322,https://doi.org/10.1016/j.oneear.2021.04.021. (https://www.sciencedirect.com/science/article/pii/S2590332221002402)

Escrig-Olmedo, E.; Fernández-Izquierdo, M.Á.; Ferrero-Ferrero, I.; Rivera-Lirio, J.M., Muñoz-Torres, M.J. (2019). Rating the Raters: Evaluating how ESG Rating Agencies Integrate Sustainability Principles. Sustainability, *11*, 915. https://doi.org/10.3390/su11030915

EU, European Commission. (2021). Overview of sustainable finance. European Commission. Available at https://ec.europa.eu/info/business-economy-euro/banking-and-finance/sustainable-finance/overview-sustainable-finance_en (Accessed: 6.10.2023)

Europe Sustainable Development Report. (2022). https://eu-dashboards.sdgindex.org/ (Accessed: 28.10.2023)

Friede, G., Busch, T. & Bassen, A. (2015). ESG and financial performance: aggregated evidence from more than 2000 empirical studies *Journal of Sustainable Finance and Investment*, *5*(4), 210–233, https://doi.org/10.1080/20430795.2015.1118917

Furrer, B., Hugenschmidt, H. (2000). Financial Services and ISO 14001, The challenge of determining indirect environmental aspects in a global certification, in R. Hillary (Ed.), ISO 14001 Case studies and pratical experience, 1st edn, Routledge.

Goldstein, D. (2001). Financial sector reform and sustainable development: the case of Costa Rica. *Ecological Economics*, *37*(2), 199–215.

GreenBiz. (2023). Charlotte Bancilhon, 5 ways financial services companies can turn SDGs into opportunities https://www.greenbiz.com/article/5-ways-financial-services-companies-can-turn-sdgs-opportunities (Accessed: 28.10.2023)

Griffiths, J. (2018). Financing the Sustainable Development Goals (SDGs), *Development*, *61*(1), 62–67.

Huang, C.-L., Vause, J., Hwong-Wen Ma & Chang-Ping Yu. (2012). Using material/substance flow analysis to support sustainable development assessment: A literature review and outlook, *Resources, Conservation and Recycling*, *68*, 104–116. https://doi.org/10.1016/j.resconrec.2012.08.012.

Huang, S.Z., Sadiq, M. & Chien, F. (2023). The impact of natural resource rent, financial development, and urbanization on carbon emission. *Environ Sci Pollut Res*, *30*, 42753–42765. https://doi.org/10.1007/s11356-021-16818-7

Huang, L., Dong, D., Dong, X. (2023). Natural resources extraction, financial expansion and remittances: South Asian economies perspective of sustainable development, *Resources Policy*, *84*, 2023, 103767. https://doi.org/10.1016/j.resourpol.2023.103767.

IMF. (2022). Goel R., Sustainable Finance and financial stability, IMF eLibrary, www.elibrary.imf.org.

IMF. (2023). https://www.imf.org/en/Topics/SDG/sdg-financing (Accessed: 28.10.2023)

Inderst, G., & Stewart, F. (2018). Incorporating environmental, social and governance (ESG)factors into fixed income investment. World Bank Group publication, p. 41

Keefe, J. (2011). From Socially Responsible Investing to Sustainable Investing. Green Money J. http://www.greenmoneyjournal.com/article .mpl?newsletterid\protect$\relax\protect{\begingroup1\endgroup\@@ over4}$41&articleid\protect$\relax\protect{\begingroup1\endgroup\@@ove r4}$544 (Accessed 03.06.2023).

Kumar, S., Sharma, D., Rao, S. et al. (2022). Past, present, and future of sustainable finance: insights from big data analytics through machine learning of scholarly research. *Ann Oper Res.* https://doi.org/10.1007/s10479 -021-04410-8

Lencucha, R., Kulenova, A. & Thow, A.M. (2023). Framing policy objectives in the sustainable development goals: hierarchy, balance, or transformation? *Global Health* 19, 5

Makarenko, Y. Yelnikova, A. Lasukova, A.R. Barhaq. (2018). Corporate social responsibility of financial sector institutions in the light of sustainable development goals financing: the role of banks and stock exchanges. *Public and Municipal Finance*, 7(3), pp. 1–14. doi:10.21511/pmf.07(3).2018.01

Niemczyk R., (2017). Concept of sustainable finance, [in] Sfera finansowa wobec wyzwań zrównoważonego rozwoju, editor M. Ziolo & K. Raczkowski, CeDeWu, Warsaw, pp. 10–16

Nizam E., Ng A., Dewandaru G., Nagayev R., & Abdulrahman N. (2019). The impact of social and environmental sustainability on financial performance: A global analysis of the banking sector. *Journal of Multinational Financial Management*, Volume 49, Pages 35–53, ISSN 1042-444X, https://doi.org/10 .1016/j.mulfin.2019.01.002.(https://www.sciencedirect.com/science/article/ pii/S1042444X18300215)

Orlitzky, M., Schmidt, F. L., & Rynes, S. L. (2003). Corporate social and financial performance: A meta-analysis. *Organization Studies*, 24(3), 403-441. https://doi.org/10.1177/0170840603024003910

ORSE (2012). How to integrate ESG risk into financial sector's operational risk management methods? Observatoire de la Responsbilitie Societale des Enterprises, September 2012. https://www.orse.org › fichier (Accessed 30.05.2023)

Pisano, U. M. & Bruckner, B. (2012). *The Financial Sector and Sustainable Development: Logics, Principles and Actors, ESDN Quarterly Report N. 27,* p. 27.

Rahi, A.F., Akter, R. Johansson, J. (2022). Do sustainability practices influence financial performance? Evidence from the Nordic financial industry, *Accounting Research Journal*, Vol. 35 No. 2, pp. 292–314. https://doi.org/10 .1108/ARJ-12-2020-0373, https://www.emerald.com/insight/content/doi/10 .1108/ARJ-12-2020-0373/full/html

S&P Global Ratings (2018). https://maalot.co.il (Accessed 30.05.2023)

Sachs, J. D. (2015). Goal-based development and the SDGs: Implications for development finance. *Oxford Review of Economic Policy*, 31(3–4), 268–278

Scholtens, B. (2006). Finance as a Driver of Corporate Social Responsibility. *Journal of Business Ethics*, 68(1), 19–33.

Stampe, J. (2014). Wildlife Fund, Environmental, social and governance integration for banks: A guide to starting implementation, Switzerland, Gland.

Sun W., Louche C., Perez R. (2011). Finance and Sustainability: Towards a New Paradigm? A Post-Crisis Agenda, Emerald Group Publishing Limited, pp. 1–325.

UN Sustainable Development Group, 2023; https://unsdg.un.org/resources/unlocking-sdg-financing-findings-early-adopters (Accessed: 28.10.2023)

UNEP FI (2019). https://www.unepfi.org/annual-review-2020/ (Accessed 30.05.2023)

Velte, P., Stawinoga, M. (2017). Empirical research on corporate social responsibility assurance (CSRA): A literature review. *J Bus Econ*, 87, 1017–1066. https://doi.org/10.1007/s11573-016-0844-2

Viederman, S. (2009) The semantics of responsible investing. FA Green, September Issue. http://www.financialadvisormagazine.com/component /content/article/14-features/4448.html?Itemid\protect$\relax\protect{\ begingroup1\endgroup\@@over4}$143 (Accessed 03.06.2023).

Vogt, M., Weber, C. (2019). Current challenges to the concept of sustainability. *Global Sustainability*, 2, E4. doi:10.1017/sus.2019.1

Wang, M. L., & Phillips-Fein, K. (2023). Environmental, Social, and Corporate Governance: A History of ESG Standardization from 1970s to the Present.

WCED. (1987). Brundtland Report, Our Common Future, World Commission on Environment and Development.

Weber O., (2018) The Financial Sector and the SDGs Interconnections and Future Directions, CIGI Papers No. 201, Centre for International Governance and Innovation

Zhan, J.X., & Santos-Paulino, A.U. (2021). Investing in the Sustainable Development Goals: Mobilization, channeling, and impact. *J Int Bus Policy* 4, 166–183

Ziolo M. (2023). Financial markets and climate change. Dilemmas and challenges versus sustainable development goals, *Studia BAS*, 2(74)

Ziolo, M., Bak, I., & Cheba, K. (2021). The role of sustainable finance in achieving Sustainable Development Goals: does it work? *Technological and Economic Development of Economy*, 27(1), 45–70

4. The banking sector and the Sustainable Development Goals (SDGs)

Ewa Kulińska-Sadłocha

4.1 SUPPORTING THE SDGs THROUGH BANKS

Banks are among some of the most important institutions in the economy. They have exclusivity in the processes of money creation, carry out the allocation and transformation of financial resources, and influence the social division of labor. Banks act as financial intermediaries – they collect savings, finance the needs of households and the activities of business entities, carry out monetary settlements, offer a range of services to manage financial risks, etc. In carrying out these tasks, banks influence the volume and pace of capital allocation, and in the case of the function related to financial advice in the broadest sense – they shape the investment decisions of entrepreneurs and influence the ways and directions of investing financial surpluses as well as the consumption behavior of households. Depending on the degree of financialization, including, in particular, the ratio of banked to unbanked or underbanked consumers, banks have a significant impact on either limiting or increasing various types of financial problems and, consequently, socio-economic problems (Kulińska-Sadłocha, Szambelańczyk, 2015).

The activities of banks are among the most regulated in the economy. Supervisory authorities, on the one hand, aim to protect depositors and the stability of the entire banking sector. On the other hand, they serve to build and consolidate public confidence in banks. Trust is crucial in banking activities, both for an individual bank and for the banking system as a whole. It is formed on the belief that an institution absolutely adheres not only to the law, but also to good standards and practices. The specific nature of the intermediation function, along with the regulatory environment and customer trust, accounts for the important role of banks in profiling the behavior and attitudes of both the population and business entities . It has allowed banks to become entities of vital importance to the successful implementation of sustainable development, since the very inception of the concept (UNEP FI, 1997; UNEP FI, 2011). From the beginning, too, the level of involvement of individual banks in this regard (i.e., the implementation of the Sustainable Development Goals) has varied greatly (Weber, 2018, pp. 4–5; Valls Martinez et al., 2020). These differences emerged due to, among other things, different approaches of bank managers and owners to the concept of sustainable development, varying awareness of the material impact of environmental, social and corporate governance factors on business operations, and differences between national regulations on environmental and social issues.

Following the announcement of the Sustainable Development Goals (SDGs) in 2015 and the adoption of the Paris Climate Agreement, sustainable development has become a priority for many countries, and the biggest challenge has been securing financing for its implementation. International organizations, countries, central banks and regulators have intensified efforts to build a sustainable financial system as well as to normalize and coordinate the activities of banks and provide financing for regional or national sustainable development strategies . Along these lines, they have set standards, formulated guidelines, issued recommendations, and finally shaped good practices at the global, regional, national and individual bank levels. All regulations refer more or less to the SDGs and the Paris Agreement, in particular defining the instruments and measures necessary for their implementation (Figure 4.1).

Global initiatives and commitments have intensified national and cross-border efforts to transform economic models to sustainable ones, as well as efforts to involve banks more broadly in the implementation of the SDGs and, above all, to provide financing. The process of transforming economies requires mobilizing the necessary financial resources, while at the same time limiting their allocation to projects with negative environmental and social impacts (Weber, 2021). The European Union has dedicated two special strategies to sustainable development: the European Green Deal and the Strategy for Financing the Transition to a Sustainable Economy. Two action plans have also been developed: the Action Plan: Financing Sustainable Growth and the European Green Deal Investment Plan. The EU is leading the way in the Environmental, Social and Governance regulatory movement with the most ESG-related

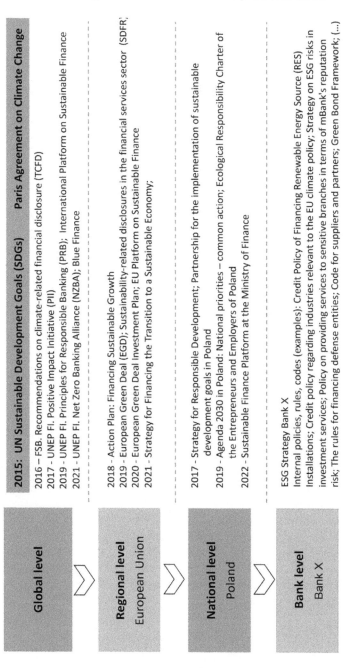

Source: Own elaboration.

Figure 4.1   *Timeline and examples of SDGs initiatives on a global, regional, national, and bank level*

issuances.[1] It is responsible for all ESG-related issuances made globally in the last five years (Cube Global, 2023). SDGs and sustainable finance are on the Polish Government's agenda and are specified, for example, through the Strategy for Responsible Development and the Agenda 2030 in Poland: National priorities – common action. Sustainable development in Poland has been driven primarily by EU legislation as well as financing from the EU Funds.

While no regulations mandate companies or banks to fully meet the SDGs, they stimulate actions that benefit a significant portion of stakeholders and promote incorporating social and environmental goals into business strategies (vision, mission, value system), internal policies, principles, and codes.

The location and functions of banks in the socioeconomic system determine the realization of the SDGs (Figure 4.2).

In achieving the SDGs, banks have a dual role: as direct implementers of the goals and as supporters of goal achievement. Supporting the realization of the SDGs entails both internal (appropriate adjustment of business models) and external actions resulting from stakeholder expectations (Zioło, 2023, pp. 55–54). The scope and strength of banks' influence depends mostly on the financial potential and organizational solutions in a given environment, including the pursuit of corporate social responsibility (CSR).

Banks contribute to the achievement of the SDGs through efficient deposit-credit and investment operations. In this way, they can eliminate, or at least effectively reduce, practices incompatible with the SDGs and stimulate sustainable entrepreneurship (Houston, Shan, 2022). Banks' impact on achieving the SDGs occurs through, among other things (Zioło et al. 2021; Carè and Weber, 2023):

- mobilizing private (long-term) capital to finance sustainable development,
- creating an offer of products and services for social groups excluded from the banking system for various reasons,
- financing activities and investments that are in line with the goals of the SDGs,
- promoting sustainable practices among clients and providing advisory services in this regard,

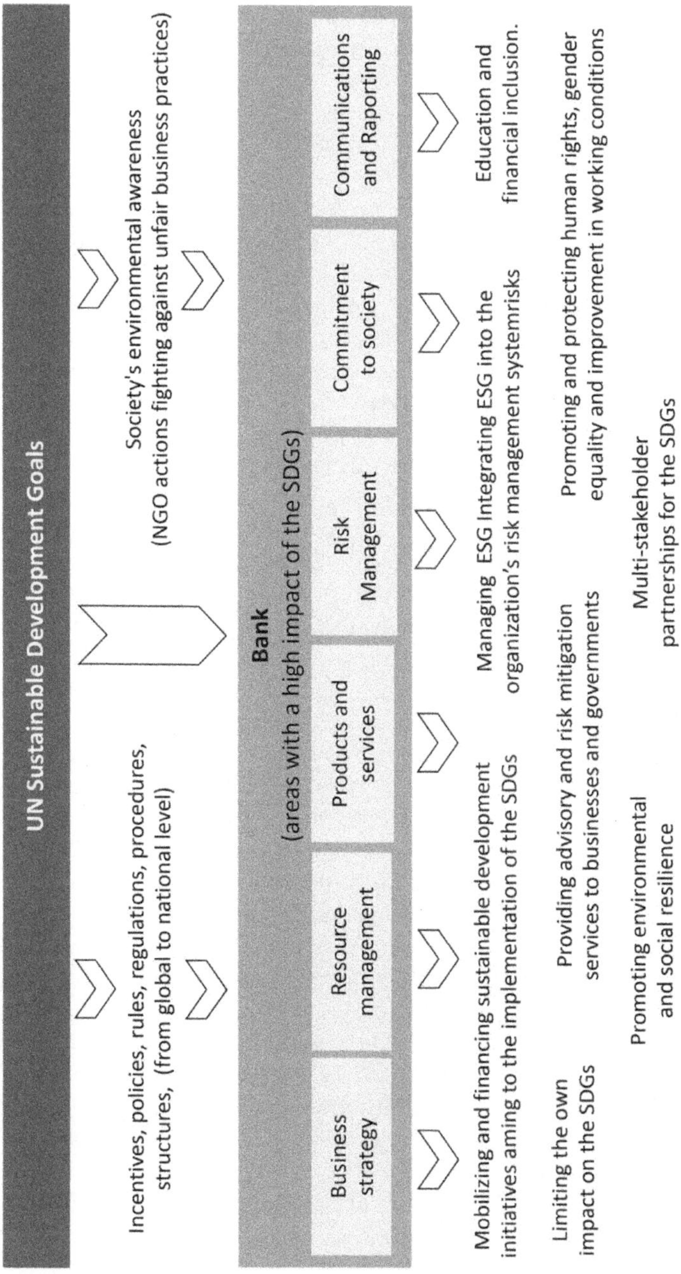

Source: Own elaboration.

Figure 4.2   *Systemic perspective on SDGs implementation in banking*

- managing risks for sustainable development (environmental, social and governance risks – ESG risks) and risk mitigation services to businesses and governments,
- conducting information, education and promotional activities on the SDGs and the related sustainable financial instruments offered.

Banks, by their actions, can create and disseminate sustainable patterns and standards of behavior and bring about a better understanding of sustainability among those around them (Inácio, Delai, 2022). Banks can also contribute to achieving the SDGs in the area of managing their own resources necessary for their business (e.g., through economical use of energy, water, paper, fuel, toners, etc.), by reducing their own greenhouse gas emissions, efficient waste management, as well as technological and organizational innovation, respect for human and labor rights, or creating appropriate working conditions. The realization of the SDGs within the bank's internal processes is an important condition for promoting these goals to customers, as well as for forming relationships with external stakeholders (e.g., through community engagement and philanthropic activities aimed at education and financial inclusion, and by engaging in multi-stakeholder partnerships for the SDGs). Banks' particular impact on the SDGs materializes through mitigating ESG risks. By managing these risks, banks can strengthen their credit and investment portfolios and mitigate these risks for customers and consumers.

The realization of the SDGs is facilitated by sustainable banking services and products, which make it possible to attract and utilize the savings of the population and business entities, as well as redirect private investment in ventures that achieve the Sustainable Development Goals. Banks are creating a whole suite of sustainable loan, account, investment and intermediary services and products aimed at meeting customer needs while supporting the achievement of the SDGs (Kunhibava et al. 2018). These include environmental and social loans on special terms (for those meeting ESG standards); microloans and accounts for the poor and excluded; affinity cards linked to ESG goals; sustainable hedging transactions (e.g., ESG risk hedging derivatives, e.g. weather derivatives); the issuance of sustainable financial instruments (certificates of deposit, savings certificates, bonds, mortgage bonds); the offering of investments in instruments issued by sustainable entities as well as in funds consisting of instruments issued by companies manufacturing products that meet ESG standards (Kulińska-Sadłocha, 2022, pp. 320–325).

Banks, by designing an appropriate product offering and applying procedures with a regard for the environment, on the one hand, can meet the expectations of customers and, on the other hand, can fulfill the role of an "educator" or even "supervisor" of the entities they finance and invest in. The bank's positive influence on consumer behavior, or even disciplining customers, supports the elimination of production and consumption patterns that disrupt sustainable development, promotes lifestyles and consumption that protect the environment, and raises awareness of environmental and social problems (Stauropoulou et. Al., 2023). It is the awareness and behaviors of consumers and producers that play a fundamental role in the transition towards a more sustainable economy – one that is more respectful of the environment, communities and the needs of future generations (Taneja, Ali, 2021).

4.2 UN PRINCIPLES FOR RESPONSIBLE BANKING

Of vital importance to the sustainable bank model are the UN Principles for Responsible Banking (PRB), adopted in September 2019, which recognize the key role of the banking sector in achieving the SDGs and are the world's foremost sustainable banking framework (Figure 4.3).

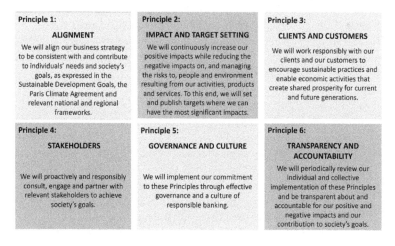

Source: UNEP FI: https://www.unepfi.org/banking/more-about-the-principles/ (Accessed: 22.10.2023).

Figure 4.3   *UN Principles for Responsible Banking*

The PRBs apply to all areas of a bank's operations, levels and management divisions (strategic, portfolio, transactional). They require signatory banks to align their core strategy, decision-making, lending and investment with the SDGs, and international agreements such as the Paris Climate Agreement. The principles focus on setting targets (environmental and social) in areas where banks have or can have the greatest impact on the SDGs. They require signatory banks to publicly report on the results of their impact and contribution to society's goals, as well as their progress in implementing the PRB and engaging key stakeholders in the process.

At the end of October 2022, 325 banks were signatories to the PRB and they had total assets of almost USD 90 trillion, which accounted for almost 50% of global banking assets. 113 member banks have participated in the Net-Zero Banking Alliance (NZBA), an accelerator program for financing ambitious climate action. They have commited to align their lending and investment portfolios to net-zero emissions by 2050 (Table 4.1). In addition, seven banks have joined the Sustainable Blue Economy Finance Initiative. The Principles promote the implementation of SDG 14: Life Below Water, and set out ocean-specific standards, allowing the financial industry to mainstream sustainability of ocean-based sectors. 33 banks have joined to PRB Commitment to Financial Health and Inclusion, which aims to accelerate action for universal financial inclusion and financial well-being of all individuals.[2]UNEP FI's report on the advancement of PRB implementation by member banks[3] shows that all have published reports in this regard fulfilling their obligation under PRB Principle 6. In addition (UNEP FI, 2023):

- 98% of banks have provided evidence of implementing effective governance and transparency to ensure sustainability in their organizations (PRB Principle 5),
- 94% of banks have aligned business strategies with the needs of individuals and social goals (PRB Principle 1),
- 94% of banks gave examples of working with customers, clients and stakeholders to encourage sustainable practices for people and the planet and to achieve the SDGs (PRB Principles 3 and 4),
- 77% of banks set two areas of impact, and 38% set two public goals related to their areas of significant positive or negative impact (PRB Principle 2).

Table 4.1   Signatories of the UN Principles for Responsible Banking and their main impact areas

Region	Number of signatories banks	Countries most represented in the PRB (Number of banks)	Assets of banks (USD trillion)	Main impact area of banks (Top 5)
Africa & Middle East	31	Nigeria (7) Egypt (7) South Africa (5)	1,3	1 Climate change mitigation 2 Financial health and inclusion 3 Inclusive, health economics 4 Diversity and gender equality 5 Decent work
North America	12	USA (6) Canada (6)	5,3	1 Climate change mitigation 2 Financial health and inclusion 3 Diversity and gender equality 4 Affordable housing 5 Inclusive, health economics
Latin America & Caribbean	52	Colombia (8) Mexico (8) Ecuador (7)	1,9	1 Climate change mitigation 2 Financial health and inclusion 3 Inclusive, health economics 4 Diversity and gender equality 5 Climate change adaptation
Asia Pacific	67	China (23) South Korea (12) Japan (9)	37,9	1 Climate change mitigation 2 Financial health and inclusion 3 Inclusive, health economics 4 Resource efficiency and circular economy 5 Biodiversity/nature

Region	Number of signatories banks	Countries most represented in the PRB (Number of banks)	Assets of banks (USD trillion)	Main impact area of banks (Top 5)
Europe	172	Norway (21) Sweden (19) United Kingdom (14)	43,2	1 Climate change mitigation 2 Financial health and inclusion 3 Inclusive, health economics 4 Biodiversity/nature 5. Resource efficiency and circular economy
Total	334		89,6	1 Climate change mitigation 2 Financial health and inclusion 3 Inclusive, health economics 4 Diversity and gender equality 5 Resource efficiency and circular economy

Source: Own elaboration based on: UNEP FI, https://www.unepfi.org/banking/bankingprinciples/prbsignatories/#_ftn1(Accessed: 31.10.2023), and UNEP FI, Responsible banking: Towards Real-world Impact. The second biennial progress report on implementation of the UN Principles for Responsible Banking, September 2023, https://www.unepfi.org/industries/banking/prb-2nd-progress-report/ (Accessed: 10.11.2023).

Actions by 87% of PRB signatories focused mainly on the climate area (SDG 13 Climate action and SDG 7 Affordable and clean energy), reflecting the growing risks in this area. Significantly fewer banks identified areas such as financial health and inclusion,[4] inclusive, health economics (SDG 3 Good health and well-being), diversity and gender equality (SDG 5 Gender Equality and SDG 8 Decent Work and Economic Growth),[5] resource efficiency and circular economy (SDG 12 Responsible consumption and production) as priority impact areas.

The banks' priority areas of influence vary regionally. Mitigating negative climate change is a priority for all member banks in North America, for 95% in Europe and 91% in the Asia-Pacific region. And while climate change mitigation for banks is also important in other regions (Latin America and the Caribbean for 64% of member banks, Africa and the Middle East for 60%), significantly more banks prioritize issues such as financial health and inclusion (45%) and social issues (53%). There is also variation in priorities between countries in a given region, and also, naturally, between individual banks in a given country. Thus, European member banks, considering their financing of entities in sectors with high greenhouse gas emissions and the number of EU climate and climate risk regulations, focus primarily on climate change mitigation. With Western European member banks leading the way on biodiversity/nature, and Scandinavian banks on resource efficiency and circular economy (UNEP FI, 2023). From a report on the practices of banks in supporting and implementing the SDGs published in June 2021 by the European Banking Federation (EBF) and KPMG Spain, it appears that European banks focused the most attention on the SDGs that address economic growth and decent work (SDG 8), climate action (SDG 13), clean energy (SDG 7), sustainable cities and communities (SDG 11) and responsible consumption and production (SDG 12). Of the 49 banks surveyed, 32 were signatories to the PRB (EBF and KPMG, 2021).

The variation in priorities is determined by the level of socioeconomic development, challenges, as well as regional or local priorities in the economic and social areas, cultural conditions, regulatory requirements, and public awareness of sustainable development.

4.3 SDGs IN THE BANK MANAGEMENT

Global challenges, society's expectations, and the growing number of sustainable development regulations are multidimensionally influencing banks' activities, mobilizing them to change their business models

(Tan et al, 2017). Socio-economic sustainability and combating climate change requires every bank to identify its impact (both positive and negative) on society's goals and integrate environmental, social and labor issues into its business strategies and practices (Figure 4.4).

Banks commonly put the ESG concept into practice by setting strategic and operational goals in the areas of environmental, social, governance, as well as taking into account the most pressing sustainability issues. It is a standard practice for banks to use the GRI (Global Reporting Initiative) methodology to assess the materiality of key environmental, social and governance issues affecting their operations. The complexity and dynamic nature of sustainability issues requires systematic improvement in the analysis of the positive and negative impact of banks (and their portfolios) on business and the financing of social needs. This includes, for example, updating the segmentation of customers and adjusting the range of products and services available to them, taking into account the specifics of location (geographic location, level of development, etc.). Banks prioritize those sustainable activities where they can have the greatest positive impact while reducing the negative impact on the SDGs. The impact of products and services on society shall also be analyzed, along with the extent to which these products directly help achieve societal goals.

It is very important to rationalize the achievement of the set goals, i.e. to identify the benefits, costs, risks and expected results associated with the bank's involvement in the SDGs (Coleton et al., 2020). Rationalization of the costs of providing banking services via remote communication channels that reduce, among other things, the so-called "carbon footprint" (materials, travel, facilities), as well as measures to reduce financial exclusion, is becoming increasingly important. Practical implementation of these goals entails, for example, undertaking economic or financial education campaigns, facilitating the use of digital technologies, etc.

Effective management of SDGs implementation also requires the modernization of banking procedures, and both in the technical-technological layer of the infrastructure and the competence-motivation layer of human resources in order to develop the intellectual capital of the bank (Anielak-Sobczak, 2023, pp. 52–55). Progress in achieving the goals must be regularly monitored (among other things: through general and specific KPIs) and reported, and decision-makers should learn from the reports and make necessary changes and adjustments. Realizing the SDGs requires the full involvement of all members of the organization

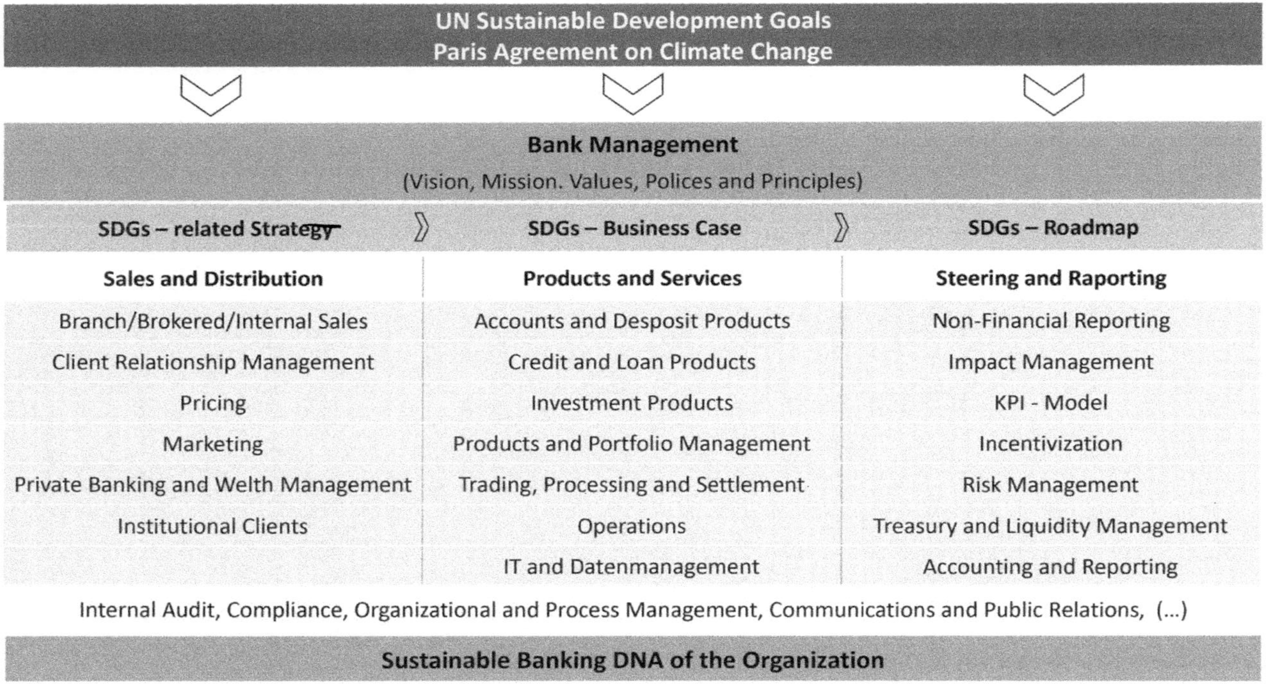

Source: Own elaboration based on: PwC Nachhaltigkeit – Sustainable Finance, https://www.pwc.de/en/sustainability/sustainable-finance .html (Accessed: 30.06.2023).

Figure 4.4 Sustainable business bank model

from governing bodies to rank-and-file operational staff. Success factors in this regard include a transparent accountability system, as well as an incentive system, including equal pay. All the more so when achieving short-term benefits, including profits, most often runs counter to achieving long-term SDGs.

The manner and scale of integration of the SDGs into a bank's strategy is driven by the individual assessment of the relevance of each motivator, as well as the barriers and constraints to integrating these issues (and the ability to overcome them). Thus, a bank can adapt in a minimal way only to regulatory requirements, or introduce new products and services in response to the demand reported by existing customers, or target new customer segments in pursuit of business opportunities, or –finally– opt for a new business model fully aligned with the path of sustainable development and actively supporting the achievement of the SDGs.

4.4 POLISH BANK PRACTICES IN SUPPORTING AND IMPLEMENTING THE UN SDGs

At the end of September 2023, the Polish sector consisted of 29 commercial banks (17 of which were foreign majority banks), 492 cooperative banks and 34 branches of credit institutions and foreign banks. The balance sheet total of the entire banking sector was about EUR 639.9 billion, with loans (53.6%) and debt instruments (32.5%) accounting for the largest share in the asset structure, and deposits (72.2%) and own issues (8.9%) in the liability structure. The financial situation of the Polish banking sector has been stable for many years (NBP, 2023), as evidenced by the relatively high supervisory indicators above the required minimums (liquidity, capital adequacy or leverage ratios), as well as the financial results achieved. In the last two years, the basic gross profitability ratios have improved significantly (at the end of 2022, they amounted to ROE –6.82%, while ROA –0.45%) (KNF, 2023).

Commercial banks in Poland, since the 1990s, have undertaken various social and environmental activities, learning to function in the realities of a market economy. Key, however, was the low level of capitalization as a result of the lack of secular capital accumulation typical of developed financial markets. Also inadequate to the realities were staff competence, technology or procedures corresponding to revolutionary changes in the economic system. Due to the rapidity of change, not all solutions developed in market economies were directly applicable in Poland. The backwardness of industrial and environmental standards also presented

Poland with much greater or even dramatic challenges in relation to the countries of the so-called old European Union. An institutional manifestation of addressing the challenges with regard to the environment was the establishment - at the beginning of the system transformation in 1990 – of Bank Ochrony Srodowiska S.A. (BOS Bank). On the other hand, various underdevelopment, especially technological underdevelopment, created great opportunities for a leap in development.

An illustration of the current involvement of banks in Poland in the implementation of the SDGs into practice is provided by information in non-financial reports (such as management board report, ESG, CSR or sustainability). The analysis was limited to reports of 10 banks listed on the Warsaw Stock Exchange, which was dictated by the availability and wide range of published non-financial information on ESG issues.[6] Of the banks analyzed, only one is a signatory to the UN PRB (mBank). In the case of 6 other banks, the signatories are their majority shareholders, mainly global banks. These banks refer to both the UN PRB and the practices in the group of which they are part. Nine of the 10 banks analyzed declare support and implementation of the SDGs, tying the goals set under the ESG concept to the SDGs (Table 4.2).

Poland's largest bank with a majority stake held by the State Treasury (Bank PKO BP[7]) is the only one that does not formally refer to the SDGs, although in its reports one can find goals and actions that contribute to the implementation of the global Agenda 2030. Three banks declare commitment to all SDGs, and two of them additionally highlight priority goals (marked in Table 4.2). Activities for SDG 4 (Quality education), SDG 5 (Gender equality) and SDG 13 (Climate action) are reported by all banks analyzed. SDG 8 (Decent work and economic growth) is also important in the activities of eight banks due to the promotion of socio-economic goals, as is SDG 7 (Affordable and clean energy) which is related to the promotion of affordable clean energy. The fewest banks declare support for: SDG 2 (Zero hunger), SDG 6 (Clean water and sanitation) and SDG 14 (Life below water). Reports published by various organizations on the level of achievement of the SDGs point to areas that need to be intensified in the country. Thus, the OECD report shows that Poland still faces challenges in improving adult skills (SDG 4) and greening the economy (mainly SDG 7 and SDG 13) (OECD, 2022). In contrast, the Eurostat report points to the need to intensify efforts under the goals related to eliminating hunger (SDG 2 Zero hunger) and responsible consumption and production (SDG 12 Responsible consumption and production) (Eurostat, 2022, p. 333). While four of these goals are of

Table 4.2   SDG in analyzed bank in Poland

Bank name	SDG No.																
	1	2	3	4	5	6	7	8	9	10	11	12	13	14	15	16	17
Alior Bank	x	x	x	x	x	x	x	xx		x		x	x	x	x	x	x
Bank Handlowy	x	x	x	x	xx	x	xx	xx	xx	x	xx	x	xx	x	x	x	xx
Bank Millennium	x	x	xx	xx	xx	x	x	xx	xx	x	x	x	xx	x	x	x	xx
Bank Pekao SA				x	x		x	x	x	x	x	x	x		x		x
BNP Paribas Polska	x	x	x	x	x	x	x	x	x	x	x	x	x	x	x	x	x
BOS Bank			x	x	x		x	x	x	x	x	x	x		x		
ING Bank Śląski	x		x	x	x		x	x	x	x	x	x	x	x	x	x	x
mBank	x		x	x	x		x	x	x	x	x	x	x			x	x
PKO BP																	
Santander Bank Polska			x	x	x			x	x	x	x		x				x

Source: Own elaboration based on disclosed non-financial information and websites of the banks listed on the Warsaw Stock Exchange.

significant importance to banks, contributions to achieving SDGs 2 are claimed by only three of banks. This means that banks in Poland do not recognize problems or opportunities for impact in this area.

It is not insignificant, as far as the implementation of sustainable development principles, to belong to international or global banking groups, which is the case for six of the banks analyzed. Thus, Santander Bank Polska, as a subsidiary of the global Santander Bank, implements the SDGs that are most consistent with its group business activities and which it has the greatest impact on implementing as a bank. With its business model based on two pillars: corporate culture and sustainable finance (Figure 4.5).

The banks analyzed are rather lightly involved in global initiatives, but the majority shareholders of Polish institutions own shares in many of them, which also translates into strategies and internal procedures. Banks' ESG, sustainability or CSR strategies are an integral part of their business strategies and usually cover a period of 2 to 3 years, the exception being a 5-year strategy. All banks declare the integration of sustainability goals with ESG issues and business strategy. These relate to:

- climate responsibility (reducing carbon footprint, supporting customers' energy transition),
- supporting the transformation of customers' business models towards sustainability,
- concern for customers' financial well-being (including ensuring equal access to services),
- caring for the environment,
- broad social and labor issues.

The banks typically organize the goals set within the framework of implementing the sustainable development principles and the actions taken towards their implementation according to ESG areas, which comes, among other things, from the widely adopted basic reporting standard – GRI (Table 4.3).

In each of the banks analyzed, areas of significant environmental, social and employee impact are identified annually, with engagement from stakeholders (in line with GRI standards). Financial and non-financial metrics (KPIs) are also used and monitored and reported. The objectives and measures analyzed show a high degree of similarity, although it is possible to identify some that take into account national and even local

Corporate Culture

Strengthening the SPF culture
Diversity
Simplifcsation
Speak Up culture

SDG 5   Gender equality
SDG 8   Decent work and economic growth
SDG 11 Sustainable cities and communities
SDG 17 Partnerships for the goals

Sustainable Finance

Green Bank

Taking care of the environment in both international external activities

SDG 3   Good health and well-being
SDG 9   Industry, innovation and infrastructure
SDG 11 Sustainable cities and communities
SDG 13 Climate action
SDG 17 Partnerships for the goals

Green Bank

Green offer

Inclusive Banking

Integrating persons at risk of exclusion into the world of banking services. Educating local communities and supporting continuous learning.

SDG 4   Quality education
SDG 5   Gender equality
SDG 8   Decent work and economic growth
SDG 9   Industry, innovation and infrastructure
SDG 17 Partnerships for the goals

Bank for persons with disabilities/ senior citizens

Bank toilored to specyfic needs of customers

Financial education at every stage of life

Santander Bank Polska Foundation – social and voluteering projects

Santander Universidades (global level)

Source: Own elaboration based on https://esg.santander.pl/2020/en/raport-2020/zarzadzanie/odpowiedzialna-bankowosc/nasze-podejscie-do-zrownowazonego-rozwoju/ (Accessed: 30.06.2023).

Table 4.3   *Examples of actions of Polish banks to implement ESG goals*

Area	Objectives
Environmental (E)	• increase financing of environmental projects (mainly renewable energy sources) • expansion of investment offerings for clients based on ESG criteria • increasing the share of ESG products (loan products secured by green real estate) in clients' portfolios • developing consulting on ESG issues affecting clients' business models • implementing changes in the organization's operations leading to minimizing the negative impact of operations on the environment • environmental education of clients, employees and the public • establishing partnerships and supporting pro-environmental initiatives within the framework of programs supporting the transformation towards a sustainable economy)
Social (S)	• offering innovative services and products and supporting innovation • providing simple and transparent communication • providing products dedicated to financing the reconstruction of post-war Ukraine by Polish companies • promoting preventive health care among employees and customers • respecting labor and human rights • creating friendly workplaces and conditions for employee development • supporting the development of mathematics education in Poland • ensuring accessibility of services for people with disabilities • charitable and philanthropic activities

Area	Objectives
Governance (G)	• ensuring responsible sales of products and services and responsible marketing (self-regulation in this regard) • ensuring the security of transactions, services and customer data • managing ESG risks in the bank's operations and customers • promoting equality and diversity and ensuring transparent remuneration policies at all levels of the organization • ensuring compliance with ESG regulations • integrating ESG objectives into management incentive systems • improving performance in ESG ratings

Source: Own elaboration based on disclosed non-financial information and websites of the banks listed on the Warsaw Stock Exchange.

specificities and activities. In this respect, banks with majority domestic capital stand out (Alior Bank, Bank Pekao, BOS Bank, PKO BP). These include, in particular, the fight against smog, support for social mobility, mathematical and financial education of the population (especially children and young people), digital competence of senior citizens or, more recently, preparation of support for the participation of Polish companies in the post-war reconstruction of Ukraine.

All banks have established organizational units (departments, divisions, offices, teams) or positions to deal with sustainability issues. Boards, committees or coordinators for ESG or sustainability issues are also established. These cells are located high up in the banks' organizational hierarchy. Most often, they are subordinated directly to the chairman of the board of directors, which indicates their rank in the organization. There is a diversity of solutions, with a visible standardization among banks with majority foreign capital, influenced by their position in the capital structure. The actions of many of the banks go beyond the regulatory requirements, with targets that are mandatory to meet and affect the annual evaluation of operational staff. In three banks, they also influence bonus systems for management.

The operationalization of the SDGs is most evident in the offering of sustainable products and services, mainly loans, although examples of investment, savings and payment products can also be identified (Table 4.4).

Table 4.4   *Examples of catalogue of sustainable products and services – the case of the BNP Paribas Bank Polska Group*

Group of products	Products and services	Segment
Products with a positive environmental impact – intended for green investments and projects	• Green Loan • Green Bond	Corporate Customers
	• EIB (European Investment Bank) credit Line Leasing • Tech loan • Investment loan with Biznesmax guarantee • ECO-COMPANY with Profit programme • Green Energy investment loan	Corporate Customers SME Customers
	• UNIA+ investment loan	SME Customers
	• Agro Progres • Insurance of renewable Energy sources (as part of the Generali Gospodarstwo Rolne)	Food & Agro Customers Micro farmers
	• Investment Loan • Green Energy investment Loan	Food & Agro Customers
	• Agro Rzeczówka Light Loan • Agro Lider	Micro farmers
	• UNIA+ investment loan • Leasing and Auto Plan with Arval for electric cars + the possibility of using the "MY electric programme" in both cases • "Green Offer" leasing and leasing loan for photovoltaics and heat pomps	Micro farmers Micro enterprises
	• ECO-COMMUNITY with profit programme • Investment loan with a BGK (polish development bank) bonus	Housing communities and associations

Group of products	Products and services	Segment
	• Instalment loan for green energy souces • Loan for green changes • Green Mortgage • Loan with subsidy from the "Clean Air Programme" • Long-tern rental of equipment financed by an instalment loan	Individual Customers
Products with a positive social impact	• Social Loan • Social Bond	Corporate Customers
	• Account Open to Non-Profit Business • Offer for Social Economy Enterprises	Housing communities and associations
Products linked to an entity's ESG rating/ performance	• Sustainability-Linked Loan • ESG Rating-Linked Loan • Sustainability-Linked Bond • Sustainability-Linked Factoring • Sustainability-Linked Hedging	Corporate Customers
	Sustainable investment products (based on ESG criteria)	Individual Customers

Source: Own elaboration based on: BNP Paribas Bank Polska Group, Management Board Raport, p. 58-59, https://www.bnpparibas.pl/en/investor-relations/stock-exchange-reports/periodic-reports (Accessed: 10.11.2023).

Among the sustainable finance products, one can point to the wide range of offerings directed to:

- companies – both loans for investments and for current operations, as well as leasing, factoring, (e.g. loans: dedicated to sustainable investments including RES investments, linked to SDGs, for companies supporting sustainable development, for the purchase of energy-efficient machinery, for the purchase of green cars, etc.).
- of the population – cash and installment loans, (e.g. for the purchase of equipment and installations aimed at reducing energy consumption, for the production of renewable energy, for the purchase of green vehicles) and leasing and Green Mortgage.

The sustainable financing offered by the banks is characterized by reduced margins, repayment grace period, lower or no commission, simplified procedures, flexible repayment schedule, etc. Each bank offers financing or co-funding from external funds, e.g. from EU funds or regional development banks (e.g. loans for entrepreneurs with non-refundable subsidies), or loans subsidized by government programs for individual customers: "My Electricity" and "Clean Air". Banks recognize the benefits and take advantage of the opportunities created by cooperation related to the distribution of external funds (especially public funds). The offer of financing is mainly directed towards environmental objectives, with a small degree of social objectives.

In the range of investment products, the banks offer, among others: sustainable investment funds, green certificates, investment advice on sustainable investments or portfolio management services for sustainable financial instruments. They emphasize responsible sales of investment products covering both distribution channels and staff competence. Only six of the ten banks analyzed have an offer of sustainable deposit products and this is much more modest in the banks than in the financing and investment offerings. It is dominated by accounts and deposits with a customer incentive component for preferred social behavior (mainly for children and young people and people 60+).

Banks also raise funds to finance sustainable/green projects from green or sustainable bond issues (mBank, PKO BP, Santander Bank Polska) and mortgage bonds (mortgage banks: PKO BP, ING Bank Slaski). In 2019, the mortgage banks' green mortgage bonds were the first green debt issues in Poland. The banks also offer other sustainable services and products. These are mainly card products (cards: made of recycled plastic, virtual, linked to the fulfilment of the SDGs), advisory services, often in online form (also in sign language), or a water footprint calculator. The analysis shows that there is a definite lack of products for customers excluded from the banking system, or in a difficult situation, in the banks' balanced offers, excluding the offer for Ukrainian citizens. All banks – in line with the regulators' recommendations (EBA, 2022; KNF 2022) – have prepared special service packages for Ukrainian refugees providing them with free access to basic payment services and improving the distribution of financial support intended for them.

Effective action for sustainable socio-economic development or against climate change, requires responsible management of human resources with respect for diversity, as well as limiting the bank's direct impact on environmental and social issues. An analysis of the measures taken by banks to reduce their direct impact on the environment and society made it possible to identify several areas of particular interest to banks, relating to reducing their own CO_2 emissions, electricity, paper and water consumption, and waste management. Banks are trying to reduce their negative impact on the environment through rational resource management, the introduction of pro-environmental and pro-social management solutions (including ISO and EMAS systems), or encouraging employees to become actively involved in bank activities. Five banks hold Green Office or LEED Gold certificates confirming that buildings meet specific environmental criteria, most often for single or several buildings (BOŚ, Santander Bank Polska, Bank Handlowy, Millennium, ING Bank Śląski). All banks calculate and monitor their own greenhouse gas emissions.[8] Some also estimate indirect GHG emissions in the value chain. Banks' financial intermediation activities are characterized by a limited supply chain. Nevertheless, they shape their collaboration with partners in terms of ESG issues: purchasing and co-operation policies with suppliers, supplier selection procedure, standard of conduct or ethics for suppliers. It is also becoming a standard to include mandatory clauses on ESG issues in contracts with suppliers.

All reporting banks disclose the consideration of ESG factors in bank risk management. They indicate the impact of these factors on credit risk as standard, to a lesser extent on operational, market, liquidity, reputation, in the case of one bank, also on legal risk. Banks use different arrangements for organizing ESG risk management (including organizational structure), standardizing the analysis of these risks, albeit in different aspects. ESG risk management processes themselves are only just being developed and refined in banks.

Social engagement and employee-related activities occupy the most space in the banks' reports, which is mainly due to the long-standing tradition of being assessed by the environment through this prism. This type of activity, compared to, for example, the creation of a service offering for people excluded from the financial system, in principle does not generate risk, is less costly and, above all, more spectacular. Community involvement is carried out to a considerable extent by bank foundations sponsoring projects within the framework of corporate social responsibility (CSR). A shift in priorities is evident in the 2022 reports. Banks have focused most attention on aid activities for Ukrainian citizens who emigrated to Poland after the outbreak of war, as well as those who decided to stay in the country.

Table 4.5 Sustainable ratings of the analyzed banks

Bank	WIG-ESG Index	Sustainable ratings				
		Sustainalytics	MSCI ESG	FTSE Russell ESG	Sustainable Fitch Ltd.	Rating V.E
Alior Bank	x	32,9				
Bank Handlowy	x	21,5				
Bank Millennium	x	23,6	A			
Bank Pekao	x	26.5	BBB	3,3		47
BNP Paribas Polska	x	10,2				
BOS Bank		14,2				
ING Bank Śląski	x	17,9			Level 2	
mBank	x	13,0	A			
PKO BP	x	23,5	A	3,3		46
Santander Bank Polska	x	19,5	A			

Source: Own elaboration based on: disclosed non-financial information, websites of the analyzed banks and Sustainalytics, https://www .sustainalytics.com/esg-ratings (Accessed: 16.11.2023).

The commitment of the analyzed banks to sustainable development activities is assessed by the market environment in both national and international ESG/CSR rankings, indices, and rating agency assessments (Table 4.5).

All banks have ESG Risk Ratings from the Sustainalytics agency[9] and the shares of nine are included in the responsible WIG-ESG index.[10] BNP Paribas Polska has the best Sustainalytics rating of 10.2. This rating signifies a low risk of a material negative impact of governance, environmental and social factors on this bank's business. Only ING Bank Slaski has an ESG rating assigned by the Sustainable Fich agencies of 2 on a five-point scale, where level 1 indicates the best rating. In addition, two banks (mBank and Bank Pekao) score well in the Bloomberg Gender-Equality Index, which takes into account large listed companies actively seeking gender equality in the working environment.

Poland's commitment to achieving climate goals and reducing greenhouse gas emissions should result in a favorable legislative and regulatory environment for building a sustainable banking sector, including tax and regulatory incentives. The war in Ukraine and, earlier, the Covid-19 pandemic, disrupted the achievement of the SDGs, including the energy transformation. These events also forced banks to reorient themselves from environmental to social issues. Banks were forced to revise their goals related to moving away from financing traditional energy sources and using energy from renewable sources in their activities. They also temporarily returned to financing the coal and coke trade. As part of the modification of the strategy, they took into account the support for investments of Polish companies in the post-war reconstruction of Ukraine and the specific needs of a new group of clients, i.e. war refugees from Ukraine.

A review and analysis of the information disclosed by analyzed banks allows us to conclude that in terms of declarations and forms, the issue of sustainable development occupies a prominent place, and its institutionalization is visible both in organizational structures and operational activities. Although the objectives and typical activities are similar, the detailed solutions are specific. Basically, it can be noted that the stimulator of the adopted goals and solutions are external regulations, which are creatively developed in individual banks or at the level of global groups and implemented to companies in Poland. This applies to both management policies and procedures, as well as the identification of the potential for the development of new or innovative products consistent with the concept of sustainable development.

4.5 BANKS' CONTRIBUTION TO THE IMPLEMENTATION OF SDGs – CRITICAL REMARKS

Sustainability is now one of the pillars of banks' business strategies, driven by new regulations and initiatives for the transition to a sustainable economy, in line with the Paris Agreement and the implementation of Agenda 2030. There is no doubt that the penetration of the concept of sustainability into banks' operations – as a rule – resulted both from initiatives taken internationally and their regional, national or local implementation, as well as from these institutions' efforts to shape a favorable image in broad segments of society against the background of a generally not so positive perception of banks. The extent and pace of banks' adaptation to the principles of sustainable development has not been equal in different locations around the world. This is due to a number of factors related to the level of socio-economic development and national wealth, as well as the activity of the banks themselves. At the same time, banks' stakeholders with the particular position of owners and investors have a significant influence.

And while banks claim to be actively involved in achieving the SDGs, many of them are very pragmatic in their approach to implementing SDG activities. Banks that are part of global financial groups adopt the practices of the parent company, often omitting – as in the case of banks operating in Poland – to adapt to the specifics and needs of the country in which they operate. Also, not all countries prioritize sustainable development and have policies that favor banks' actions towards the SDGs. This is particularly true of less developed economies that rely on environmentally unfriendly industries. In this situation, without financial assistance from countries and banking sectors with higher levels of development, it is very difficult to change this state of affairs and the realization of the SDGs is seriously threatened (Gallagher, Yuan, 2017). Due to the high uncertainty of future profits, banks are reluctant to finance entities operating in underdeveloped countries about which they have very limited information. On the other hand, the loans offered to such entities are characterized by high cost, even several times higher than in developed countries (UN Inter-agency Task Force on Financing for Development, 2022, pp. 27–28). On top of this, there is still a focus in many banks on activities that primarily guarantee good financial results. This results in money that could be used to finance sustainable business ventures or customer needs ultimately being involved in various types of financial instruments, often non-bank and high risk. Changing this situation requires an overhaul of the institutional environment of the financial sphere, not only in terms of its impact on the sustainability of economic entities, but also in terms of eliminating opportunities for financial speculation and returning banks to a servant role to the real economy.

Banks' focus on short-term business effects means that they often overlook or fail to see the long-term benefits of sustainability due to the higher degree of uncertainty. Financing the transition to a sustainable economy requires banks to make a long-term commitment, and this involves acquiring long-term sources of refinancing. For example: in the case of Polish banks, long-term loans have been financed with short-term and current deposits as standard for many years. To date, neither the market nor the discussions held so far on this issue have led to a solution to the problem.

Banks have a much greater impact on achieving the SDGs through their financial activities than their internal processes. However, reports of the analyzed banks largely focus on the organization's internal resources, as well as commitment to society (CSR). It is extremely rare for banks to disclose negative impacts on the SDGs, except for mandatory disclosures (e.g., EU Taxonomy, SFRD). On the basis of reported data, it is difficult to make an objective assessment of the level of banks' commitment to achieving the SDGs, which is due to, among other things: the descriptive nature of many indicators that have varying information capacity, as well as the use of inconsistent measurement principles and methods, estimated quantities, or even units of measurement (e.g., paper consumption measured in sheets, riffles or kilograms). The lack of comparability also applies to assessments by rating agencies, which use different methodologies to evaluate banks' sustainable exposure. On top of this, a huge number of rankings and competitions result in numerous banks reportingabout being a leader in sustainable banking. The rankings are created according to different criteria, often incomparable, resulting in a bank being a leader in one ranking, ranking next in others or even not being ranked.

The concept of sustainable development and its operationalization in the ESG is civilization's response to identified threats to planet Earth and, in less catastrophic terms, to the broader global social order. Unfortunately, the lack of consensus among scientists and especially politicians on the extent and pace of possible perturbations to humanity in general or to individual continents limits decisive remedial action. Achieving the SDGs requires cooperation among all those contributing to and benefiting from economic development. Achieving the goals requires support from governments through appropriate legislation and initiatives to encourage and support the private sector, including banks in particular, in their efforts to achieve the SDGs (Sardianou et al., 2021).

NOTES

1. In-force regulation, rules, legislation, consultations, policies, etc.
2. The UN PRB Commitment to Financial Health and Inclusion launched in December 2021 and is a first-of-its-kind commitment to promote universal financial inclusion and foster a banking sector that supports the financial health of customers. https://www.unepfi.org/banking/commitments/commitment-to-financial-health-and-inclusion/ (Accessed: 31.10.2023).
3. This second biennial report, coming at the end of the initial four-year implementation phase, relies mainly on data from the signatories of the PRB that have made it to the halfway mark of the implementation phase. It synthesizes individual reports from 245 member banks that joined between 2019 and 2022, representing 75% of all member banks as of 30 June 2023.
4. Financial health and inclusion are directly linked to six SDGs, including SDG 1 (No Poverty), SDG 5 (Gender Equality), SDG 8 (Decent Work and Economic Growth), SDG 9 (Industry, innovation and infrastructure), SDG 10 (Reduced inequalities) and SDG 17 (Partnerships for the goals). (UNEP FI, 2022).
5. Diversity and gender equality are important components of the SDGs. Primarily, they relate to SDG 5 (Gender Equality), aiming ensure equal opportunities for all, irrespective of gender, age, race, ethnicity, origin, religion, economic status, or disability, and SDG 8 (Decent Work and Economic Growth), which also embodies the values of diversity, calling for equal pay for work of equal value and promoting safe and inclusive working environments.
6. In March 2021, the Council of the Warsaw Stock Exchange adopted new corporate governance rules included in the "Best Practices 2021". They indicated the need to take ESG issues into account in corporate governance structures, including: measurable ESG goals as part of business strategies and planned activities and progress in its implementation determined using financial and non-financial measures. And although the application of corporate governance principles is voluntary, all analyzed banks reported their application (GPW, 2021).
7. Bank PKO BP SA is the oldest and the largest bank in Poland in terms of assets (over 17% of the balance sheet total of the banking sector).
8. Banks declare to reduce their negative impact on climate change, commit to achieving full climate neutrality by 2050, and in relation to their own emissions, they indicate much shorter deadlines, e.g. Millennium by 2027; ING Bank Śląski until 2030.

9. A rating range of 0–10 indicates negligible risk; 10–20 low risk; 20–30 medium risk; 30–40 high risk; above 40 – severe risk. And although BOS Bank has a rating of 14,2, which means low risk, it is not included in the WIG-ESG index because it is not a participant of the WIG20 and mWIG40 indices (one of the selection criteria to the WIG-ESG index).

10. WIG-ESG index has been calculated since September 3, 2019 based on the value of portfolio of companies recognized as socially responsible, i.e. those that comply with the principles of socially responsible business, in particular in the field of environmental, social, economic and corporate governance issues (ESG). The WIG-ESG Index is derived largely from reports by Sustainalytics, a research firm (Morningstar Company) that provides ESG data for the world's largest investment and index companies (GPW, 2023, p. 11).

REFERENCES

Anielak-Sobczak K. (2023). *Kapitał intelektualny a konkurencyjnoś ć banków w Polsce*, Wydawnictwo Uniwersytetu Łódzkiego, Łodź 2023.

Carè R., Weber, O. (2023). *Sustainable Finance: Banks, Sustainability, and Corporate Financial Performance.* In: Dion, M. (eds) Sustainable Finance and Financial Crime. Sustainable Finance. Springer, Cham, pp 41-61,https://doi.org/10.1007/978-3-031-28752-7_3

Cube Global. (2023). *The evolution of ESG regulation*, March, www.cube.global/wp-content/uploads/2023/03/CUBE-Data-Report_The-Evolution-of-ESG.pdf (Accessed: 25.10.2023).

Coleton A., Brucart M.F., Gutierrez P., Le Tennier F., Moor C., *Sustainable Finance: Market Practices*, EBA Staff Paper Series, No. 6, January 2020, www.eba.europa.eu/sites/default/files/document_library//Sustainable%20finance%20Market%20practices.pdf (Accessed: 18.11.2023).

da Silva Inácio L., Delai, I. (2022). *Sustainable banking: a systematic review of concepts and measurements.* Environ Dev Sustain 24, pp. 1–39 (2022). https://doi.org/10.1007/s10668-021-01371-7.

EBA (2022), EBA calls on financial institutions to ensure compliance with sanctions against Russia following the invasion of Ukraine and to facilitate access to basic payment accounts for refugees, https://www.eba.europa.eu/eba-calls-financial-institutions-ensure-compliance-sanctions-against-russia-following-invasion#:~:text=EBA%20calls%20on%20financial%20institutions%20to%20ensure%20compliance,basic%20payment%20accounts%20for%20refugees%2011%20March%202022 (Accessed: 10.11.2023).

EBF and KPMG. (2021). *European bank practices in supporting and implementing the UN Sustainable Development Goals*, June, https://www.gruppobcciccrea.it/Documents/Sostenibilita/European%20bank%20practices%20Report.pdf . (accesed: 12.11.2023).

Eurostat (2022). *Sustainable development in the European Union – 2022 monitoring report on progress towards the SDGs in an EU context*, https://ec.europa.eu/eurostat/documents/15234730/15242025/KS-09-22-019-EN-N

.pdf/a2be16e4-b925-f109-563c-f94ae09f5436?t=1667397761499 (Accessed: 15.11.2023).

Gallagher, K. P., Yuan, F. (2017). Standardizing Sustainable Development: A Comparison of Development Banks in the Americas. *The Journal of Environment & Development*, 26 (3), 243-271. https://doi.org/10.1177 /1070496517720711

GPW. (2021). *Dobre praktyki spółek notowanych na GPW 2021*, 2021, https:// www.gpw.pl/pub/GPW/files/PDF/dobre_praktyki/DPSN21_BROSZURA .pdf (Accessed: 10.11.2023).

GPW. (2023), Indices GPW Benchmark, September, https://gpwbenchmark.pl/ en-karta-indeksu?isin=PL9999998955 (Accessed: 16.11.2023).

Houston, J., Shan, H. (2022). *Corporate ESG Profiles and Banking Relationships. The Review of Financial Studies*, Volume 35, Issue 7, July 2022, pp. 3373–3417, https://doi.org/10.1093/rfs/hhab125 (Accesed: 22.10.2023).

KNF (2022). Komunikat UKNF z 4 marca 2022 r. w sprawie oferty produktowej dla uchodźców z terenów objętych działaniami wojennymi w Ukrainie, https://www.knf.gov.pl/knf/pl/komponenty/img/Komunikat_dot_stanowiska _KNF_ws_uslug_bankowych_dla_uchodzcow_z_Ukrainy_77363.pdf (Accessed: 12.11.2023).

KNF. (2023), *Informacja na temat sytuacji sektora bankowego w 2022 roku*, https://www.knf.gov.pl/knf/pl/komponenty/img/Sytuacja_sektora _bankowego_raport_roczny_2022_85174.pdf (Accessed: 16.11.2023).

Kulińska-Sadłocha E., Szambelańczyk J (2015), *Lokalne instytucje kredytowe w koncepcji zrównoważonego rozwoju Polski*. In Sektor finansowy. Stymulatory i zagrożenia rozwoju, K. Pietraszkiewicz (ed.), PTE, Warszawa. pp. 240-266.

Kulińska-Sadłocha E. (2022). *W jaki sposób banki mogą wspierać transformację gospodarki w kierunku modelu zrównoważonego?* In W poszukiwaniu zielonego ładu, M. Burchard-Dziubińska (ed.), Wydawnictwo Uniwersytetu Łódzkiego, Łódź 2022, pp. 311–332.

NBP. (2023). *Financial stability Report*. June, https://nbp.pl/wp-content/uploads /2023/07/Raport-o-stabilnosci-systemu-finansowego-06_2023-EN-WWW .pdf (Accessed: 16.11.2023).

Kunhibava S, Ling, S., Ruslan, M. K. (2018). *Sustainable financing and enhancing the role of Islamic Banks in Malaysia*. Arab Law Quarterly, 32, pp. 129–157.

OECD. (2022). *Measuring Distance to the SDG Targets – Poland 2022*, https:// www.oecd.org/wise/measuring-distance-to-the-SDG-targets-country-profile -Poland.pdf (Accessed: 15.11.2023).

PwC Nachhaltigkeit – Sustainable Finance, https://www.pwc.de/en/sustainability /sustainable-finance.html (Accessed: 30.06.2023).

Sardianou E., Stauropoulou A., Evangelinos K., Nikolaou I. (2021). A materiality analysis framework to assess sustainable development goals of banking sector through sustainability reports. Sustainable Production and Consumption. Volume 27, July 2021, Pages 1775–1793

Stauropoulou A., Sardianou E., Malindretos G., Evangelinos K., Nikolaou I. (2023). The effects of economic, environmentally and socially related

SDGs strategies of banking institutions on their customers' behavior. World Development Sustainability, Volume 2, June. Elsevier

Tan L. H.,, Chew B. CH., Hamid S. R. (2017). A holistic perspective on sustainable banking operating system drivers: A case study of Maybank group. Qualitative Research in Financial Markets, Vol. 9 No. 3, pp. 240-262. https://doi.org/10.1108/QRFM-12-2016-0052

Taneja S., Ali L. (2021). Determinants of customers' intentions towards environmentally sustainable banking: Testing the structural model, Journal of Retailing and Consumer Services. Volume 59, March, https://doi.org/10.1016/j.jretconser.2020.102418

UN Inter-agency Task Force on Financing for Development. (2022), *Financing for Sustainable Development Report* 2022, https://developmentfinance.un.org/fsdr2022 (Accessed: 20.11.2023).

UNEP FI (1997), *Statement by Banks on the Environment and Sustainable Development* (as revised – may 1997), https://www.unepfi.org/fileadmin/statements/fi/fi_statement_en.pdf (Accessed: 25.10.2023)

UNEP FI (2011), *Statement of Commitment by Financial Institutions (FI) on Sustainable Development*, https://wedocs.unep.org/bitstream/handle/20.500.11822/42662/Committment_financial_institutions.pdf?sequence=1&isAllowed=y (Accessed: 18.11.2023).

UNEP FI. (2022). *Financial Inclusion and Financial Health Target Setting*, September, https://www.unepfi.org/wordpress/wp-content/uploads/2022/09/PRB-Guidance-Financial-Inclusion-2.pdf (Accessed: 13.11.2023).

UNEP FI. (2023) *Responsible banking: Towards Real-world Impact. The second biennial progress report on implementation of the UN Principles for Responsible Banking.* September, https://www.unepfi.org/industries/banking/prb-2nd-progress-report/ (Accessed: 10.11.2023).

Valls Martínez MdC, Cruz Rambaud S., Parra Oller I.M (2020). Sustainable and conventional banking in Europe. PLoS ONE 15(2): https://doi.org/10.1371/journal.pone.0229420

Weber O. (2021). The banking sector and the SDGs: interconnections and future directions. In A Research Agenda for Social Finance, pp 175–198.

Weber O. (2018), *The Financial Sector and the SDGs Interconnections and Future Directions.*

CIGI Papers No. 201. November, https://www.cigionline.org/static/documents/documents/Paper%20No.201web.pdf (Accessed: 30.09.2023).

Weber O., Feltmate B. (2016). *Sustainable Banking. Managing the Social and Environmental Impact of Financial Institutions.* University of Toronto Press, Toronto.

Zioło M., Spoz A., Kulińska-Sadłocha E. (2021) *Zrównoważone rynki finansowe.* Perspektywa krajowa i międzynarodowa. Warszawa: PWE.

Zioło M. (2023). *Rynki finansowe wobec zmian klimatu. Dylematy i wyzwania a cele zrównoważonego rozwoju.* In *Gospodarka, rynek i społeczeństwo wobec zmian klimatu, K. Marchewka-Bartkowiak and M. Sobolewski* (eds.) Studia BAS, No 2 (74), pp. 43–66.

5.   Insurance sector and SDGs

Anna Spoz

5.1 THE INSURANCE SECTOR'S CONTRIBUTION TO THE SUSTAINABLE DEVELOPMENT GOALS

The insurance sector plays an important role in the economy. It is the main source of long-term capital, being one of the largest institutional investors (International Monetary Fund, 2016), and by diversifying the risks of business entities and households, it contributes to the financial stabilization of individual entities and the economy as a whole.

Insurance companies, being part of the financial sector, have a certain specificity. The essence of their activity is to exchange unpredictable financial risk for a specific, fixed cash contribution. Insurance companies are obliged to ensure their solvency and the ability of policyholders to pay out invested funds at any time, hence their resources must be invested conservatively. Insurers have a fiduciary duty to maintain or increase the value of "policyholder" assets (Pfeifer and Langen, 2021), which naturally limits their options for investment strategies. Additional restrictions on investments result from legal provisions (The Geneva Association, 2018). Insurance regulatory authorities impose capital charges on investments depending on the value of the risk incurred, assuming that the riskier the investment, the higher the capital charge. The purpose of such action is to ensure an adequate level of capital to cover insurers' liabilities. Regulations in this area vary in individual countries or regions (Pfeifer and Langen, 2021).

It should be noted here that individual industries, and within industries, individual business entities are exposed to various types of risks of varying intensity. Therefore, the conditions for concluding insurance, the amounts and deadlines for payment of premiums, and payment of claims vary depending on the type of insurance. Therefore, insurers differ in the way they manage financial risk related to assets and liabilities. In the case of life insurers, the aim of the investment is to generate predictable and stable income while guaranteeing cash flows at an appropriate level and shaping liabilities at a predictable level. Hence, it is important to match the structure of assets and liabilities, and interest rate risk becomes a key issue. Insurers offering non-life insurance are focused on investing funds in more liquid investments and with shorter payback periods (usually lasting from one to three years) (BaFin, 2020). Also in this case, interest rate risk is very important.

Due to its specific nature, the insurance sector plays a significant role in helping individual countries achieve sustainable development goals in the areas of economic growth, social inclusion, and environmental protection (Holliday et al. 2021) (Figure 5.1).

In the dimension of environmental protection, the insurance sector contributes to the implementation of sustainable development goals through the appropriate structure of assets and liabilities of individual insurance companies. In this dimension, insurers can influence the achievement of the following sustainable development goals: SDG6 (Clean Water and Sanitation), SDG12 (Responsible Consumption and Production), SDG 15 (Life on Land), SDG 7 (Affordable and Clean Energy), SDG 13 (Climate action), SDG 14 (Life Below Water), SDG 1 (No Poverty), SDG 3 (Good Health and Well-being), SDG 8 (Decent Work and Economic Growth), SDG9 (Industry, Innovation and Infrastructure), and SDG 11 (Sustainable Cities and Communities).

The activities of insurers contribute to better social inclusion by providing insurance to the most marginal social groups (including disabled people, young people, women, elderly people, and the unemployed). In this dimension, the activities of insurance companies can have a positive impact on the implementation of such sustainable development goals as: SDG 4 (Quality Education), SDG 5 (Gender Equality), SDG10 (Reduced Inequalities), SDG 16 (Peace Justice and Strong Institutions), SDG 17 (Partnership for the Goals), SDG 1 (No Poverty), SDG 3 (Good Health and Well-being), SDG 8 (Decent Work and Economic Growth), SDG 9 (Industry, Innovation and Infrastructure), and SDG 11 (Sustainable Cities and Communities).

In economic terms, the insurance sector can contribute to the implementation of the SDGs through (Holliday et al., 2021):

Acting as an investor and asset manager – influencing the allocation of capital, directing it towards sustainable projects;

Diversification and risk transfer – participating in financing/co-financing the reconstruction of property damaged/lost as a result of fortuitous

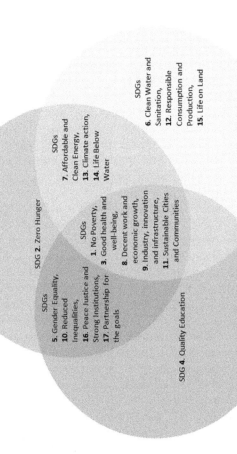

Source: Holliday, S., Remizova, I., & Stewart, F. (2021). *The Insurance Sector's Contribution to the Sustainable Development Goals (SDGs)*. World Bank Group.

Figure 5.1 Insurance sector contribution to the Sustainable Development Goals

events, including extreme weather conditions; protecting against financial losses as a result of fortuitous events; financing or co-financing the costs of medical care.

Offering employer places – insurance companies are a workplace for agents from all over the world.

In the economic area, the activities of the insurance sector directly and indirectly contribute to the implementation of the following goals: SDG 2 (Zero Hunger), SDG 7 (Affordable and Clean Energy), SDG 13 (Climate Action), SDG 14 (Life Below Water and No Poverty), SDG 1 (No Poverty), SDG 3 (Good Health and Well-being), SDG 8 (Decent Work and Economic Growth), SDG 9 (Industry, Innovation and Infrastructure), SDG 11 (Sustainable Cities and Communities), SDG 5 (Gender Equality), SDG 10 (Reduced Inequalities), SDG 16 (Peace Justice and Strong Institutions), and SDG17 (Partnership for the Goals).

The insurance sector contributes to achieving the Sustainable Development Goals through risk transfer mechanisms across households, businesses, and public sector entities (Figure 5.2).

Each transmission channel can contribute to achieving one or more sustainable development goals. In the case of households, their saving and borrowing can lead to achieving SDG 8 (Decent work and economic growth) and SDG 10 (Reduced inequalities). Providing access to credit to entrepreneurs may translate into the implementation of SDG 9 (Industry, innovation and infrastructure), and agriculture development may translate into the achievement of SDG 2 (Zero hunger). Activities of public sector entities in the field of financial stability may have a positive impact on the implementation of SDG 10 (Reduced inequalities).

The activities of the insurance sector may translate into the implementation of individual SDG goals to varying degrees. In "The Insurance Sector's Contribution to the Sustainable Development Goals (SDGs)" report, Holliday et al. (2021) differentiated the strength of the insurance sector's impact on the implementation of individual sustainable development goals (Figure 5.3).

According to the authors of the report, the insurance sector has the greatest impact on achieving the sustainable development goals in the field of Climate Action (SDG 13), Sustainable Cities and Communities (SDG 11), Good Health and Well-being (SDG 3), and Reduced Inequalities (SDG 10). A description of insurers' contribution to the implementation of selected SDGs is provided in Table 5.1.

Insurers have a strong impact on achieving goals: No Poverty (SDG 1), Zero Hunger (SDG 2), and Decent Work and Economic Growth (SDG 8)

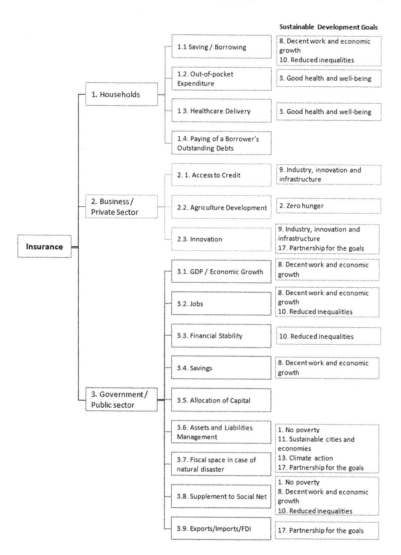

Source: Holliday, S., Remizova, I., & Stewart, F. (2021). *The Insurance Sector's Contribution to the Sustainable Development Goals (SDGs).* World Bank Group.

Figure 5.2   Transmission mechanism of insurance impact and SDGs

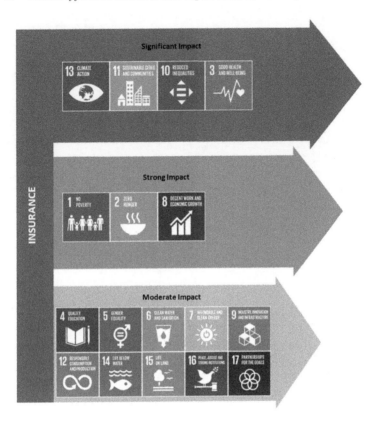

Source: Holliday, S., Remizova, I., & Stewart, F. (2021). *The Insurance Sector's Contribution to the Sustainable Development Goals (SDGs).* World Bank Group.

Figure 5.3   Impact of the insurance sector on SDGs

goals. The impact of the activities of the insurance sector as a supplier of insurance products and an institutional investor on the achievement of the above-mentioned goals is presented in Table 5.2.

5.2 REGULATION, INSURANCE SUPERVISION AND SDGS

Insurance supervision can play an important role in implementing the concept of sustainable development and achieving its goals. Thanks to

Table 5.1   *Insurance sector and selected SDGs*

Sustainable Development Goal	
SDG 13. Climate action	Within the scope of the insurance offer: <ul><li>Creating 'green insurance' or 'climate-smart insurance'</li><li>Creating products that protect the agricultural sector from risks impacted by climate change</li><li>Creating products protecting households, businesses and properties in disaster-prone areas or areas affected by climate change</li><li>Within meso- or macro-level insurance systems, creating products that protect organizations providing key services to vulnerable communities or government budgets</li><li>Incentivising or encouraging better disaster or climate risk management</li></ul> As insurance industry companies and institutional investors, insurers: <ul><li>Create active ESG frameworks addressing climate risk and adaptation.</li><li>Climate risks are incorporated in investment strategy and a part of assets invested in sustainable investments (e.g., low-carbon investments; resilience-enhancing infrastructure)</li><li>Operating conforms to or is in line with the relevant environmental/climate risk management regulatory frameworks.</li><li>Contribute to climate or disaster risk expertise through the creation of new risk finance instruments, education and awareness campaigns on disaster risk, and knowledge-sharing initiatives like the creation of open-source disaster risk data</li></ul>

Sustainable Development Goal	
SDG 11. Sustainable Cities and Communities	Within the scope of the insurance offer: • Encourage road safety for property and vehicle owners (e.g., motor insurance), proposing new ways of promoting safe driving e.g. telematics • Require or incentivize strong construction standards or property risk management for both residential and commercial buildings • Support climate adaptation of cities and urban communities As insurance industry companies and institutional investors, insurers: • Create active ESG frameworks addressing sustainable cities and communities • Share expertise with local governments on risk recognition and management in building sustainable cities • Have internal policies on sustainability for their own offices.
SDG 3. Good Health and Well-being	Within the scope of the insurance offer: • Develop products that fill the gaps in the community's public health insurance programme, commercial health insurance market, or universal private health insurance. For example, temporary disability/income protection for informal workers, SMEs, and migrant workers, low-income, rural and indigenous communities, people with pre-existing conditions or disabilities, and pandemic cover, hospital cash insurance • Encourage risk management in the provision of health services, such as vaccination programmes and hospital insurance • Promote health seeking or preventative behavior, e.g., bundled with telemedicine and other services, plans rewarding for healthy behavior, and covers last-mile costs such as ambulance fees As insurance industry companies and institutional investors, insurers: • Share their expertise in health risk in other ways beyond their core business, e.g., health awareness campaigns, contributing expertise on predictive modeling and systemic health risk to healthcare policy formulation

Sustainable Development Goal	
SDG 10. Reduced inequalities	• The role of insurance in reducing inequality is more difficult to trace based on specific insurance products. In this case, all types of insurance addressed to socially excluded groups, protecting against financial losses due to property damage or accidental events, and insurance related to health and work safety protection should be mentioned. As employers, insurers can take actions aimed at supporting employee rights, equal opportunities, counteracting discrimination, and all types of exclusions.

Source: Own elaboration based on Chiew, H. L. (2021). *Insurance and the SDGs, Access to Insurance Initiative.* https://a2ii.org/en/sustainable-development-goals (Accessed: 15.11.2023).

regulatory initiatives, supervisory authorities can influence the offerings of insurance companies so that their products, services, and investments support the implementation of sustainable development goals (mitigating climate change, transforming the economy towards zero emissions) in a way that favors social inclusion (improving the quality of life, combating poverty, particularly among older people). Insurers and pension funds, as long-term investors and entities managing social risk, have the opportunity to meet the challenges related to the implementation of the concept of sustainable development.

The European Insurance and Occupational Pensions Authority (EIOPA) through its activities supports the implementation of the concept of sustainable development. It has identified sustainable finance, digital transformation, governance, policy, risks to financial stability, and governance as part of its strategic priorities.

The key area of EIOPA's activities for 2023–2025 is sustainable financing, which enables and improves the process of transition to a sustainable economy. The focus on sustainable finance is not only about incorporating ESG factors into the prudential and behavioral framework for insurers and pension funds, but also analyzing the risks and impacts of climate-related change, biodiversity issues, and social risks.

In accordance with the regulation establishing EIOPA and the sectoral regulation on Insurance and Occupational Pensions for 2022–2024, EIOPA has designated 7 key areas of activity in the field of sustainable

Table 5.2   The insurance sector and selected SDGs

Sustainable Development Goal	
SDG 1. No Poverty	Within the scope of the insurance offer: • Creating specific product lines, e.g., life, hospitalization, personal accident, agriculture, or property. • As entrepreneurs from the financial sector, insurers: • Support research and understanding of low-income communities, with initiatives such as demand and needs surveys or protection gap research; • Industry initiatives of insurers in collaboration with policymakers to reduce poverty, e.g., national insurance schemes.
SDG 2. Zero Hunger	Within the scope of the insurance offer: • Insurance plans and products that help smallholder farmers. These can be collective policies owned by cooperatives, public entities, or the department of agriculture, or they might be individual policies held by farmers; • Products protecting providers of key services to farmers; or • Insurance against climate change or natural disasters safeguarding agricultural communities and food production. • As insurance industry companies and institutional investors, insurers: • Contribute risk expertise regarding issues related to food security, for example, by doing research and participating in policy discussions.

Sustainable Development Goal	
SDG 8. Decent Work and Economic Growth	Within the scope of the product offer, insurers may create insurance: • Intended to promote overall household resilience and financial wellbeing, e.g., products integrated with other financial services • Designed to protect MSMEs, e.g., fire or property cover, motor, agricultural or business interruption insurance, employers/public/product liability insurance, cyber insurance; • Designed for people with unstable, unregulated, or hazardous jobs with little financial security, such as gig economy and informal workers, immigrants, workers in factories or farms who handle heavy equipment and are frequently excluded, persons with impairments, MSMEs, care workers, and domestic assistants. Examples of products are personal accident, disability, and workers' compensation insurance. As insurance industry companies and institutional investors, insurers: • Contribute to GDP and employment as a whole, and employment in underprivileged communities; • Include SDG 8 as an internal target or carry out initiatives in line with SDG 8; • Have the resources to ensure equal opportunities for minorities, disabled people, and economically disadvantaged people.

Source: Own elaboration based on Chiew, H. L. (2021). *Insurance and the SDGs, Access to Insurance Initiative.* https://a2ii.org/en/sustainable-development-goals (Accessed: 15.11.2023).

finance. The identification of areas, along with the characteristics of the most important activities in each area, is included in Table 5.3.

In the area of cybersecurity, EIOPA undertakes activities aimed at supporting individual groups of entities (consumers, enterprises, supervisors) in the process of digital transformation. Examples of initiatives in this area include the Digital Operational Resilience Act (DORA) and the European Single Access Point (ESAP).

Actions are also taken to improve the quality and effectiveness of supervision, especially in the case of cross-border activities. In this

*Table 5.3   Identification of EIOPA's key areas of activity in the field
            of sustainable finance, along with key results in a given
            area*

Area of activity	Key deliverables
Including ESG risks in insurers' and pension funds' prudential frameworks	• Suggestions for supervisory climate risk reporting under Solvency II • Analysis of prudential treatment under Solvency II of assets and/or activities linked with environmental and/or social objectives or associated extensively with harm to such objectives • Report on underwriting practices and prudential treatment of the integration of climate change-related adaptation measures in non-life insurance products • Examining how IORP's fiduciary obligation incorporates sustainability factors. • Re-evaluation the standard capital charge formula for natural disaster risk
Consolidation of the macro/ microprudential risk assessment of ESG risks	• Report on analysis of physical risk • Methodological principles of insurance stress testing – climate change. • Involvement in a possible cross-sectoral stress test exercise on climate change
Promotion of sustainability disclosures and a framework for sustainably conducting a business	• Advice on how to apply sustainability-related provisions in the insurance sales process • Guidance on disclosures and reporting under the Sustainable Finance Disclosure Regulation and Taxonomy Regulation • Advise EU COM on measures to address greenwashing
Supporting supervision of ESG risks and supervisory convergence in the EU	• Guidebook on the supervision of climate risks in Solvency II Pillar 2 • Application guidelines for monitoring the use of climate change risk scenarios in ORSA, with a voluntary pilot exercise on running climate change materiality assessment and using scenarios on climate change in ORSA • Cost and Past Performance assessment of ESG products • Advice on the supervision of ESG conduct risks, including greenwashing

Area of activity	Key deliverables
Addressing gaps in protection	• Complete the dashboard on insurance protection gap for natural disasters • Analysis of customer behavior and contract terms in relation to insurance coverage for natural disasters
Promotion of the open source modeling and data in regard to climate change risks	• Analyze opportunities for the use of open source tools for modeling natural catastrophe • Develop ways to improve the acquisition of consistent, thorough insured loss data
Contribute to international convergence for the sustainability risks assessment and management	• Active and leading membership in the Network for Greening the Financial System (NGFS), the Sustainable Insurance EU-US dialogue climate-related projects on climate risk financial oversight and climate risk and resilience • Supervisors (IAIS) in areas of sustainable finance • Forum (SIF) and the International Association of Insurance

Source: Own elaboration based on: European Insurance and Occupational Pensions Authority (2023). *Sustainable finance activities 2022–2024.* https://www.eiopa .europa.eu/browse/sustainable-finance_en (Accessed: 10.10.2023).

respect, EIOPA will review supervisory materials on convergence in accordance with the Solvency II Regulation.

Taking care of the stability of the industry and protection of clients' interests, EIOPA pursues a proactive policy of identifying, assessing, monitoring, and reporting on risks in the insurance and occupational pension schemes sector. In the area of management, EIOPA ensures the increase of human capital and ensures compliance with safe working conditions and respect for human rights.

EIOPA and other European Supervisory Authorities (ESAs) received a request from the European Commission for information on the risk of greenwashing. This inquiry concerns three areas, i.e., understanding and better monitoring greenwashing and related financial risks; taking stock of the implementation and supervision of sustainable finance policies aimed at preventing/addressing greenwashing; and assessing the supervisory and enforcement response.

5.3 REGULATIONS, PRINCIPLES FOR SUSTAINABLE INSURANCE AND SUSTAINABLE/GREEN INSURANCE PRODUCTS

The shape and scope of insurers' activities are largely influenced by legal regulations. For several years now, we have been witnessing the number of legal regulations devoted to ESG issues growing year by year. The leaders in this area are Great Britain and the European Union, but other countries are also working intensively in this area. Table 5.4 contains selected legal regulations in the field of ESG affecting the activities of insurance companies in 2023.

The process of implementing the concept of sustainable development into the operations of insurance companies is difficult. The main problem is the heterogeneity of guidelines, recommendations, and regulations in this area in individual countries. This restriction is particularly evident in the case of international insurance groups that operate in different jurisdictions.

The United Nations Environment Programme Finance Initiative (UNEP FI) has developed policies to facilitate the implementation of sustainability principles in the operations of insurance companies (Table 5.5).

The growing number of extreme, difficult-to-predict weather phenomena and the losses resulting from their occurrence, as well as the complexity and dynamics of social changes, increase customer interest in sustainable insurance products. In response to consumer expectations, insurance companies are expanding their offer with sustainable insurance products. Alignment of products with ESG factors may depend on the product line, i.e., products aimed at consumers and businesses, due to the specificities of both groups and different insurance needs. Creating sustainable products is a complicated process and requires risk assessment on the part of the insurer and the insured. For example, property insurance for electric vehicles may involve higher repair costs for the insurer, and the use of renewable energy sources may require innovative risk transfer solutions.

Examples of sustainable insurance products aimed at consumers and businesses are included in Table 5.6.

The offer of insurance companies in the field of sustainable insurance products will evolve to adapt to the needs and expectations of customers. This type of insurance will certainly become more and more popular and will have a greater share in the product structure of insurance companies from year to year.

Table 5.4   *Selected legal regulations regarding ESG in selected regions*

Jurisdictions	Selected environmental-related regulations	Selected social-related regulations
UK	• Streamlined Energy & Carbon Reporting since 2019 • Prudential Regulation Authority (PRA) expectations on managing financial risk arising from climate change, set out in SS3/19, form part of a supervisory approach from 2022 • Task Force on Climate-Related Financial Disclosures (TCFD) disclosures for large companies for reporting periods from 6 April 2022, if not already caught by earlier requirements for listed companies • TCFD product and entity-level reporting for life companies with insurance-based investment products from 30 June 2023 • Anti-greenwashing requirements expected to be applicable from 30 June 2023 • Green taxonomy: UK government is expected to provide an update on timing and substance during 2023 • UK SDR CP 22/20	• Human Rights Statement (Equality and Human Rights Commission 2019) • Modern slavery reporting (2016) • Gender pay gap reporting required (Government Equalities Office, 2017) • Diversity and inclusion reporting for listed companies for reporting periods after 1 April 2022

Jurisdictions	Selected environmental-related regulations	Selected social-related regulations
EU	• Corporate Sustainability Reporting Directive (CSRD) • Sustainable Finance Disclosure Regulation (SFDR) requires product reporting on sustainability objectives • The European Union (EU) taxonomy identifies those activities that are considered as significantly contributing to six sustainability objectives from 2022 • The European Insurance and Occupational Pensions Authority (EIOPA) requires additional climate information relating to insurance products and investments from 2023 year-end quantitative reporting templates (QRTS) • EIOPA is exploring potential differential treatment in the Solvency Capital Requirement (SCR) calculation for exposures to sustainable investments and economic activities	CSRD introduces mandatory disclosure in accordance with European Sustainability Reporting Standards (ESRS) across environmental, social, and governance topics. Phased implementation will start in the financial year 2024 for the largest firms. Mandatory limited assurance is required, which also affects non-European groups with significant European businessGender Balance Directive will come into effect in June 2026Corporate Sustainability Due Diligence Directive (CSDDD) reporting may be possible from 2025
ASPAC	• Australian Prudential Regulation Authority (APRA) introduced CPG 229 (effective November 2021), setting out TCFD-aligned guidance • Hong Kong Securities and Futures Commission (HKSFC) will introduce mandatory TCFD reporting requirements by 2025 • Japan's Financial Services Agency (FSA) introduces mandatory TCFD requirements, phasing in from 2022 • China's green taxonomy, known as the 'Green Bond Endorsed Project Catalogue' was first released by the People's Bank of China (PBOC) in 2015. A revised edition was published in April 2021	• Monetary Authority of Singapore (MAS) has developed a roadmap for issuers to disclose on ESG matters from 2022
Americas	SEC will phase in climate reporting requirements from 2023 through to 2025	

Source: KPMG (2023). *ESG in insurance: Strategy and transformation.* https://assets.kpmg.com/content/dam/kpmg/xx/pdf/2023/06/kpmg-fy23-Insurance-esg-strategytransformation-final.pdf (Accessed 10.11.2023).

Table 5.5   *Principles of sustainable insurance*

Principle	Specification
Principle 1	Integrating environmental, social, and governance (ESG) considerations relevant to the insurance business into the decision-making process Possible actions: Company Strategy • Establish a company strategy at the board and executive management levels to identify, assess, manage, and monitor ESG issues in business operations • Establish a dialogue with business owners about the importance of ESG issues in the company's strategy • ntegrate ESG issues into employee recruitment, training, and employee engagement programs
	Risk Management & Underwriting 1 Establish processes to identify and assess ESG issues inherent in the portfolio and be aware of potential ESG-related consequences of the company's transactions 2 Integrate ESG issues into risk management, underwriting, and capital adequacy decision-making processes, including research, models, analytics, tools and metrics Product & Service Development • Develop products and services which reduce risk, have a positive impact on ESG issues, and encourage better risk management • Develop or support literacy programmes on risk, insurance and ESG issues Claims management • Respond to clients quickly, fairly, sensitively, and transparently at all times and make sure • claims processes are clearly explained and understood • Integrate ESG issues into repairs, replacements, and other claims services Sales and Marketing • Educate sales and marketing staff on ESG issues relevant to products and services and integrate key messages responsibly into strategies and campaigns • Make sure product and service coverage, benefits, and costs are relevant and clearly explained and understood Investment Management • Integrate ESG issues into investment decision-making and ownership practices (e.g. by implementing the Principles for Responsible Investment)

Principle	Specification
Principle 2	Collaborating with customers and business partners to raise awareness of environmental, social, and governance (ESG) issues, manage risks, and develop solutions Possible actions: Customers & Suppliers Dialogue with clients and suppliers on the benefits of managing ESG issues and the company's expectations and requirements on ESG issues Provide clients and suppliers with information and tools that may help them manage ESG issues Integrate ESG issues into tender and selection processes for suppliers Encourage clients and suppliers to disclose ESG issues and to use relevant disclosure or reporting frameworks. Insurers, reinsurers and intermediaries Promote the adoption of the Principles Support the inclusion of ESG issues in professional education and ethical standards in the insurance industry
Principle 3	Work with governments, regulators, and other key stakeholders to promote wide-ranging action in society on environmental, social, and governance issues Possible actions: Governments, regulators, and other policymakers Support prudential policy, regulatory, and legal frameworks that enable risk reduction, innovation, and better management of ESG issues Dialogue with governments and regulators to develop integrated risk management approaches and risk transfer solutions Other key stakeholders Dialogue with intergovernmental and non-governmental organizations to support sustainable development by providing risk management and risk transfer expertise Dialogue with business and industry associations to better understand and manage ESG issues across industries and geographies Dialogue with academia and the scientific community to foster research and educational programmes on ESG issues in the context of the insurance business Dialogue with media to promote public awareness of ESG issues and good risk management

Principle	Specification
Principle 4	Clear, transparent and regular disclosure of information on the implementation of sustainable insurance principles Possible actions: Assess, measure and monitor the company's progress in managing ESG issues and proactively and regularly disclose this information publicly Participate in relevant disclosure or reporting frameworks Dialogue with clients, regulators, rating agencies and other stakeholders to gain mutual understanding on the value of disclosure through the Principle

Source: UNEP FI. (2012). *PSI. Principles for Sustainable Insurance.* https://www.unepfi.org/psi/wp-content/uploads/2012/06/PSI-document.pdf (Accessed: 19.11.2023).

5.4 CHALLENGES FACING THE INSURANCE SECTOR TOWARDS SUSTAINABLE DEVELOPMENT

The role and importance of the insurance industry in achieving the Sustainable Development Goals are growing. It becomes a kind of ambassador of sustainable development, stimulating business entities to include ESG factors in their operating strategies.

The dynamics and nature of the ongoing climate and technological changes, as well as the expectations of employees and consumers, combined with macroeconomic instability, mean that in order to survive and develop, enterprises around the world need financial security, which the insurance industry can help achieve thanks to a product offer that takes into account ESG risks.

The potential of the insurance industry in this area results from the fact that insurance companies act as a "financial safety net" for particular groups of entities (enterprises, households, and public sector entities), providing them with protection against financial losses resulting from specific risks. According to the Global Risks Report (World Economic Forum, 2023), for several years, environmental and social risks have been among the top ten risks with the greatest impact in the long (10 years) and short (2 years) period.

Insurers are aware of the growing customer demand for insurance products related to sustainable development. Increasingly aware consumers also want insurance companies, in addition to developing a sustainable product offer, to function in accordance with the assumptions of this concept. Meeting these expectations requires insurers to implement appropriate solutions both at the level of the industry (legal regulations) and individual insurance companies (transformation towards sustainability).

Transformation at the entity level requires changing the operating model to a sustainable business model as well as analyzing and possibly modifying the company's portfolio. Modification of the business model towards a sustainable business model requires the inclusion of ESG factors in the decision-making processes, the implementation of appropriate, more advanced technologies, including data collection and processing, and modification of the company's structure and culture to improve working conditions and improve cooperation between employees. Customer-insurer relationships are also extremely important because companies can optimize their product offerings based on information obtained from customers. Therefore, companies are increasingly conscious and comprehensive in their approach to controlling and selecting ESG risk in their operations and portfolio management, increasing the share of sustainable insurance products in it.

The transformation of insurance companies takes place on several levels. More and more insurers are incorporating net zero emissions targets into their operational strategy. Entities that have announced such commitments within the Net Zero Insurance Alliance (NZIA) face the challenge of developing targets by 2030 in this area in line with the target setting protocol proposed by NZIA. In practice, this means for insurance companies the need to set or organize emission reduction goals, analyse the size and structure of the portfolio, and consider how to modify it. Insurers that have not yet announced net zero targets are faced with building a framework for measuring portfolio emissions and comparing the relative emissions intensity of customers.

Growing awareness of the importance of environmental issues resulted in a new global framework being agreed in 2022 to stop and reverse the degradation of the environment by 2030. Agreements in this regard at the enterprise level are still ongoing. For insurers, however, it represents a challenge to develop an environmental-based risk management framework and portfolio structure in such a way as to support the transition to an environmentally friendly economy.

Table 5.6   *Sustainable insurance products for consumers and businesses*

Product line for individual customers	
Property Renewable Energy Reimbursements	Protecting homeowners who use an alternative energy system from the effects of power outages. This type of insurance can provide compensation for:
	1 Loss of income from the sale of surplus generated energy; 2 Utility charges or official fees for inspections or permits related to the reconnection of an alternative energy system into the grid; 3 Costs of purchasing substitute electricity
Discount on devices that reduce property losses	Homeowners can receive special discounts in the form of credits for the installation of safety devices or the selection of special construction techniques in disaster-prone areas, such as the purchase of shutters to protect against extreme storms and wind
Discounts for a fuel-efficient/low-emission vehicle	Discounts for drivers of electric and hybrid vehicles
Product line for business customers	
Upgrade to a green company fleet	Option to upgrade the company's fleet to hybrid vehicles for new replacement vehicles in support of the policy
Renewable Energy Project Insurance	Helping renewable energy companies manage risk, defend against litigation, and protect assets at all stages of project delivery – from design to distribution
Modernization/replacement insurance for real estate and equipment for the renewable energy industry	Protect your business from incurring high costs due to rapid technological change in the field of renewable energy. The offer covers the costs of replacing equipment with a more energy-efficient setup. You can add equipment that is currently in use, under construction, or newly purchased to your policy

Source: Capgemini Invent. (2021). *Sustainable Insurance. How P&C insurers can protect and power our journey to a more sustainable world.* https://www.capgemini .com/wp-content/uploads/2021/04/2021-–04-12_Invent_Sustainable-insurance_ POV_A4-P_Interactive_Final.pdf (Accessed: 19.11.2023).

One of the main challenges resulting from the provisions of the Paris Agreement of 2015 is the transition to a low- and ultimately zero-emission economy. To achieve this goal, an energy transformation is undoubtedly needed, which in practice means for insurers a shift to more ecological methods of operation (e.g., through digitization of processes and document flow, use of renewable energy sources, use of energy-saving machines and devices) and responsible investments in new fuel infrastructure, fossil fuels and projects related to obtaining energy from renewable energy sources. Insurers will also have to develop effective methods of measuring and assessing the risk associated with the implementation of projects consistent with the concept of sustainable risk.

Consumer awareness of sustainable development means that investors are increasingly interested not only in the extent to which a company will reduce emissions but also in how it plans to achieve it. Regulatory authorities in the European Union, the United States, and the United Kingdom have even proposed introducing into legal regulations a requirement for companies to publish transformation plans. Insurance companies also face the challenge of developing credible transformation plans.

The legal regulations being prepared also encourage various types of enterprises (including insurers) to consider their role in supporting the process of transitioning the economy as a whole to a climate-neutral one. In this context, it is necessary to analyze the interconnections between enterprises and the impact of the actions of specific groups of entities (competitors, consumers, decision-makers) on the speed and scope of the "greening" of insurance companies, as well as the power of insurers' influence on the sustainable development of other entities.

The disclosure obligation for insurance companies results from the Sustainable Finance Disclosure Regulation, Insurance Distribution Directive, EU Taxonomy, and Non-financial Reporting Directive / Corporate Sustainability Reporting Directive. Practice shows that insurance companies make constant progress in terms of disclosures made. According to the report by the Task Force on Climate-Related Financial Disclosures (TCFD), the sector improved its overall level of climate risk disclosure from 25% to 41% over two years. Obtaining comparable ESG data would enable the classification of companies and projects in the context of sustainability and would contribute to improving the risk management process.

The obligation to disclose has intensified the phenomenon of greenwashing. Actions to limit this phenomenon are taken at the level of the European Union, the USA, and Great Britain. EU supervisory committees, including EIOPA, issued an invitation to report greenwashing. In the USA, a special task force to counteract greenwashing was established at the Securities and Exchange Commission (SEC). In order to manage assets effectively, insurers must be sure in which projects they invest and ensure that the sustainable products they offer meet the sustainability criteria.

Entities' sustainability declarations will become a source of customer classification. Increasingly, the attitude of entities towards the issue of sustainable development will determine the choice of insurance package and its price.

REFERENCES

Bundesanstalt für Finanzdienstleistungsaufsicht (BaFin). (2020). Guidance notice on dealing with sustainability risks

Capgemini Invent. (2021). *Sustainable Insurance. How P&C insurers can protect and power our journey to a more sustainable world.* https://www.capgemini.com/wp-content/uploads/2021/04/2021-04-12_Invent_Sustainable-insurance_POV_A4-P_Interactive_Final.pdf (Accessed: 19.11.2023).

Equality and Human Rights Commission. (2019). Guidance for businesses. https://www.equalityhumanrights.com/guidance/business/guidance-businesses

European Insurance and Occupational Pensions Authority. (2023). *Sustainable finance activities 2022–2024.* https://www.eiopa.europa.eu/browse/sustainable-finance_en (Accessed: 10.10.2023).

Government Equalities Office. (2023). *Gender pay gap reporting: guidance for employers.* https://www.gov.uk/government/publications/gender-pay-gap-reporting-guidance-for-employers (Accessed: 24.02.2024)

Holliday, S., Remizova, I., & Stewart, F. (2021). *The Insurance Sector's Contribution to the Sustainable Development Goals (SDGs).* World Bank Group.

International Monetary Fund. (2016). *Global Financial Stability Report.* Potent Policies for a Successful Normalization. https://www.imf.org/en/Publications/GFSR/Issues/2016/12/31/Potent-Policies-for-a-Successful-Normalization (Accessed: 12.11.2023).

KPMG. (2023). *ESG in insurance: Strategy and transformation.* https://assets.kpmg.com/content/dam/kpmg/xx/pdf/2023/06/kpmgi-fy23-Insurance-esg-strategytransformation-final.pdf (Accessed: 10.11.2023).

Pfeifer, D., & Langen, V. (2021). Insurance Business and Sustainable Development. *Risk Management,* 1–10.

The Geneva Association. (2018). *Climate Change and the Insurance Industry: Taking Action as Risk Managers and Investors. Perspectives from C-level executives in the insurance industry.* Zürich. https://www.genevaassociation.org/sites/default/files/research-topics-document-type/pdf_public/climate _change_and_the_insurance_industry_-_taking_action_as_risk_managers _and_investors.pdf (Accessed: 10.11.2023).

World Economic Forum. (2023). *Global Risks Report 2023.* https://www3 .weforum.org/docs/WEF_Global_Risks_Report_2023.pdf (Accessed: 24.02.2024).

World Economic Forum. (2023). *Global Risks Report 2023.* https://www3 .weforum.org/docs/WEF_Global_Risks_Report_2023.pdf (Accessed: 24.02.2024).

6. Strengthening SDGs through capital markets

Anna Spoz

6.1 CAPITAL MARKETS AND SUSTAINABLE DEVELOPMENT

The capital market – due to its function in the economy – may be an important element in the process of implementing the concept of sustainable development. It contributes to the mobilization and allocation of capital and its valuation. It acts as an intermediary between savers (those with surplus money) and business entities that need money to achieve a specific goal. It mediates the flow of capital and contributes to increasing the efficiency of its use. This efficiency can be considered from the point of view of savers and investors. For savers, efficiency means obtaining capital at a lower cost. From the point of view of investors, this efficiency was traditionally understood as the maximization of profits at an acceptable level of risk. For several years, as a result of the popularization of the concept of sustainable development, when making investment decisions, investors, in addition to quantitative criteria, also take into account qualitative factors, i.e., environmental, social and governance aspects. Referring to the provisions of the Brundtland Report, sustainable capital markets can be defined as capital markets that, by financing economic development, ensure that the needs of the contemporary generation are met without the risk that future generations will not be able to meet their needs (United Nations, n.d.).

The role of the capital market in promoting sustainable development can be manifested in (Stoian and Iorgulescu, 2019):

• mobilizing capital and directing it to the implementation of projects that take into account ESG aspects;

- making access to capital dependent on the issuer's inclusion of environmental, social, and corporate governance (ESG) factors in its strategy;
- influencing, through managerial supervision, the implementation of the concept of sustainable development into the application of good practices in enterprises.

The sustainable capital market is an important source of obtaining capital for investments related to the concept of sustainable development and achieving the Sustainable Development Goals (SDGs). According to the roadmap for a sustainable capital market, it contributes to the implementation of the following Sustainable Development Goals: SDG 7 (Affordable and clean energy), SDG 8 (Decent work and economic growth), SDG 5 (Gender equality), SDG 12 (Responsible consumption and production), and SDG13 (Climate action) (Figure 6.1).

The importance of a sustainable capital market is growing every year. The global market for sustainable finance (i.e., bonds, funds, and voluntary carbon markets) was estimated to be worth USD 5.8 trillion in 2022 and, importantly, investors see sustainable finance as a long-term strategy. Despite difficult macroeconomic conditions, investor interest

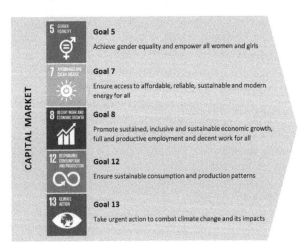

Source: Own elaboration based on https://sdgs.un.org/partnerships/roadmap
-sustainable-capital-markets#targets-tab (Accessed: 26.10.2023).

Figure 6.1   Sustainable capital market and SDGs

in sustainable funds was still greater than in traditional funds, and the value of the global sustainable funds market in 2022 was USD 2.5 trillion (United Nations Conference on Trade and Development., 2023).

Looking at the directions of capital flows, it can be seen that the following sustainable development goals are included: SDG 13 (Climate action), SDG 8 (Decent work and economic growth), and SGD 12 (Responsible consumption and production). Environmental protection projects are particularly popular, which is confirmed by the green bond market growing every year. Institutional investors show particular interest in supporting projects related to sustainable energy. The capital-intensive and long-term nature of investments in renewable energy sources corresponds to the maturity profiles of pension funds' liabilities (United Nations Conference on Trade and Development, 2023). United Nations Conference on Trade and Development (UNCTAD) data shows that more than two-thirds of reporting funds have declared to achieve net zero in their investment portfolios by 2050. To this end, they plan to phase out fossil fuels in favor of renewable energy sources.

It is worth noting here that capital markets can play an important role in supporting the sustainable transformation of economic entities. Financing is sometimes even more needed by entities preparing or in the process of transformation to a more sustainable operating model, i.e., switching to low-emission production methods. The capital market can be an extremely important source of obtaining capital for the transformation of entities operating in the so-called "brown" industries. Not all business entities can afford to switch to more "ecological" forms of doing business, and the possibility of obtaining stable and long-term sources of financing in this area may become a key factor enabling decarbonization of enterprises with high carbon dioxide emissions. Of course, pro-ecological projects should not only be identified with the issue of reducing greenhouse gas emissions, but also with counteracting the phenomena of deforestation, water shortages, soil sterilization, etc. (Scheidig, 2023). In recent years, due to the COVID pandemic and eliminating its negative effects on society and the economy, a dynamic increase in the issuance of social bonds can be observed.

In implementing the sustainable development goals, financing the transformation should cover both environmental and social projects, especially since they are often interconnected.

6.2 THE ROLE OF CAPITAL MARKETS IN FINANCING THE SDGS

Stock exchanges connect entities with financial surpluses (capital providers) with entities seeking capital, in an organized manner and based on transparent rules. They can therefore play an important role in promoting sustainable development in capital markets. Currently, there are 37 Stock Exchanges with a Green Bond Segment, while ten years ago none of the exchanges conducted activities in this area. The first stock exchange to list green bonds was the Oslo Stock Exchange (January 2015). Five months later, i.e., in June 2015, sustainable bonds appeared on the Stockholm Stock Exchange.

Stock exchanges can support the development of a sustainable capital market in several ways, primarily by acting as an intermediary between capital donors and recipients, providing issuers with access to a base of potential investors interested in financial instruments related to sustainable development. Examples of such investors may include pension funds, investment funds, insurance companies, enterprises and financial institutions, and even individuals. In this way, stock exchanges can support the mobilization of capital and its focus on the implementation of projects related to sustainable development. Thanks to a wide range of potential investors, the stock exchange, on the one hand, gives issuers the opportunity to obtain capital of higher value, and on the other hand, it brings image benefits as a socially responsible entity that combines care for achieving economic efficiency with care for the environment and society.

Trading sustainable instruments on the stock exchange increases their liquidity. In a situation of low liquidity, it is more difficult to match potential issuers of securities with potential investors, which increases the time-consuming process and also increases its costs. Thanks to the stock exchange, the relatively easy and quick access of issuers of sustainable debt instruments to potential investors and investors to sustainable debt instruments increases their liquidity.

In order to facilitate the investment process, stock exchanges create segments of sustainable financial instruments and the so-called lists of specific types of bonds related to sustainable development. In this way, they make it easier for investors to find an appropriate financial instrument and invest in projects/assets that fit the concept of sustainable development. Listing or segmenting sustainable financial instruments may also play a role in ensuring the integrity of the sustainability bond market, as issuers are most often required to disclose how they allocate proceeds from issuance and report on their use. In the future, stock exchanges may require the issuer to provide a certificate of use of funds. Although such requirements may increase the costs of the issuance process, they may contribute more to increasing investor confidence in sustainable bonds at the post-issuance stage, and thus increase the demand for them and, consequently, the price.

ESG ratings are helpful in the process of making investment decisions. For the investor, they constitute the basis for making investment decisions, significantly shortening the time of this process. Nearly 70% of investors declare that they regularly use ratings, and almost 60% of them claim that ESG ratings provide information important in the process of making investment decisions. Investors are increasingly interested in investing in companies with good ESG results. More than half of investors admit that ESG ratings are also a good complement to research on the management of ESG risks in their own organization (Oczyp and Mikiewicz, 2023). For enterprises, the assessment obtained in the rating confirms the inclusion of the concept of sustainable development in their operational strategy. By joining the ESG rating, a company can improve its relationships with stakeholders, increase investor interest, gain access to capital at a lower cost, and increase its competitive advantage. Over the last 10 years, there has been a strong correlation between companies' performance in the context of ESG factors and their investment values. Institutional investors are particularly interested in investing in low-risk companies.

ESG ratings are created by rating agencies specializing in this field. ESG rating agencies can be divided into three types (Pichola et al. 2021):

- basic data providers – offering a wide range of data that is publicly available and raw; their most common source is company reports (Bloomberg, Refinitive);
- comprehensive data providers – offering a combination of raw and publicly available data as well as data processed by agency analysts and their own questionnaires (Sustainalytics, MSCI, ISS ESG);
- specialized data providers – offering processed and highly individualized data covering a selected range of ESG (usually one or two aspects); the recipients of this type of data are investors who want to start or expand their investments in a specific scope (CDP, TruCost).

Currently, there are over 600 rating agencies operating in the market. There is no single, universal methodology for analysing ESG data used by all rating agencies, which leads to a situation where different agencies assess a given business entity differently, thus weakening the importance of the ESG rating. Most often, the basis for assessing an entity in the field of ESG is non-financial data. This allows agencies greater freedom in selecting the areas and categories examined, as well as the indicators used for evaluation. There is also no single, universal ESG assessment system. Some agencies assign ratings in a similar way to credit rating agencies (using AAA–D ratings), while others use numerical scores, with some agencies having the highest scores signifying the best rating, while in others, high scores may mean a worse rating. Agencies also differ in their area of analysis, which may cover selected companies, sectors and regions or focus on all or selected ESG aspects.

To make it easier for investors to make decisions on investments related to sustainable development, to enable investors to track the performance of green bonds, compare returns and their volatility, rating agencies, financial institutions, and international institutions launch green bond indices. Examples of such indices are: Solactive Green Bond Index, Series, S&P Dow Jones Green Bond Index, ChinaBond China Green Bond Index Series, Barclays & MSCI Green Bond Index (Climate Bonds Initiative, 2017).

The response to the growing demand of stakeholders for ESG information regarding market entities was the emerging legal regulations obliging individual groups of entities to disclose sustainability issues. The first regulation in this area was the Non-financial Reporting Directive (NFDR), which was addressed to large entities and public-interest entities. The NFDR covers an estimated 11,700 large companies and groups across the EU, including listed companies, banks, insurance companies and other companies designated by national authorities as public interest entities. The above-mentioned entities must publish information related to environmental impact, social issues and treatment of employees, respect for human rights, counteracting corruption and bribery, and diversity on company management boards (in terms of age, gender, and education).

Another directive regarding reporting is the Corporate Sustainability Reporting Directive (CSRD). Its aim is to improve sustainability reporting. Sustainability information provided by companies should be comparable, reliable, and easy to find and use by users using digital technologies.

The directive will enter into force in 2024 for large enterprises but will cover more entities in the following years.

In the financial sector, a regulation requiring financial market participants and financial advisors who provide investment or insurance advisory services in relation to insurance-based investment products to publish in writing a strategy for introducing sustainable development risks into their activities and ensuring transparency of introducing these risks is the Sustainable Finance Disclosure Regulation (SFDR). This regulation imposes new obligations on financial market participants offering investment products, including banks, in terms of transparency and disclosure of the approach to risk management for sustainable development as part of their investment activities and investment decision-making.

Although individual groups of entities complied with the disclosure obligation, the reports prepared turned out to be not very comparable. However, they intensified the greenwashing phenomenon. To standardize and specify what is meant by "sustainable" action, the EU Taxonomy was developed. Its aim is to support investors in making informed investment decisions towards more sustainable economic activity. According to the Taxonomy, an economic entity is not classified in terms of sustainability as a whole, but its individual activities are considered. For each eligible activity, it must be verified that it meets the relevant technical criteria (Technical Screening Criteria– TSC) that demonstrate a significant contribution to the objectives of climate change mitigation and/or adaptation (these two objectives currently have TSC criteria adopted) (Konfederacja Lewiatan, 2021). The criteria of the EU Taxonomy are often precise and measurable and are intended to contribute to the "greening" of subsequent activities of a company and its business partners. The implementation of the concept of sustainable development at various levels is a requirement of modern times and an expression of solidarity between current generations and future ones.

Capital markets can act as significant agents of change, but their ability to drive change depends on the balance between certainty and standardization.

6.3 DEVELOPING SUSTAINABLE CAPITAL MARKET AND SUSTAINABLE FINANCIAL INSTRUMENTS

The situation in the sustainable financial instruments market is presented in a report published by The Association for Financial Markets in

Europe (AFME), covering data from the second quarter of 2023 and previous years. According to the report, in 2022, total issuance of European ESG bonds and loan reached EUR 690 billion (Figure 6.2), decreasing by 8.9% compared to 2021 (EUR 757 billion). When comparing the first halves of years year-over-year (YoY), the decrease in 2023 (11.8%) was lower than the decrease in 2022 (14.6%). However, in Q2'2023, total issuance of European ESG bonds and loan declined by about 24% YoY.

Looking at total European ESG bonds and loan issuance in individual countries (Figure 6.3), there are significant differences between the countries occupying the first three places: France, Germany, and Italy. The fourth place, occupied by the Netherlands, is also clearly distant from the third place, but between it and the next two places (UK and Spain), the differences are minor. In further places, the total issuance is constantly decreasing, but the issuance of individual types of bonds and loans is changing. For example, in Turkey, Sustainable-Linked Loans prevail, and Denmark has a significant share of Sustainable-Linked Bonds and Transition Bonds, which other countries (apart from the top three) issue very little.

In Q2 2023, European green bond emissions decreased both in relation to Q1 2023 (QoQ) and Q2 2022 (YoY); however, in the years 2015–2020, green bonds emissions systematically increased every year (Figure 6.4). The first half of 2023 also shows an increase in emissions compared to the first half of the previous year. The annual growth was maintained despite the fact that in some periods the value of emissions decreased from quarter to quarter.

The European Social Bond issuance value was the only one to increase (+11.3%) in Q2 2023 compared to Q2 2022 (Figure 6.5). Thanks to this, it was possible to maintain growth in the first half of 2023 compared to the first half of 2022. However, the volume of emissions in 2022 was much lower than in 2021 and even lower than in 2020.

Sustainable bond issuance volumes, as well as sustainable-linked and transition bond issuance volumes, significantly decreased QoQ in Q2 2023 (Figures 6.6 and 6.7). These volumes also decreased compared to Q2 2022. Despite this, sustainable bond issuance in H1 2023 was slightly higher than in H1 2022, which did not occur in the case of sustainable-linked and transition bond issuance.

The annual volumes of European sustainability-linked and green-linked loan issuance increased from 2017 to 2021 and then decreased in 2022 (Figure 6.8). Despite an increase (+6.9%) in issuance in Q2'23 compared to Q1'23, it is unlikely that total issuance volume in 2023 will

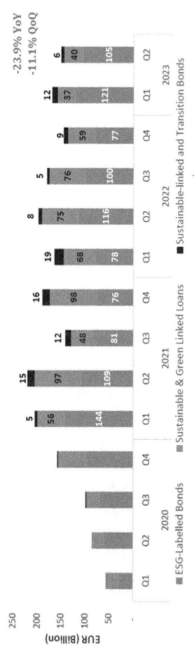

Source: The Association for Financial Markets in Europe (2023). *Sustainable Finance Report – Q2 2023.* https://www.afme.eu/Portals/0/DispatchFeaturedImages/AFME%20Sustainable%20Finance%20Report%20-%20Q2%202023—1.pdf (Accessed: 19.11.2023).

Figure 6.2   European ESG bonds and loan issuance (2020–2023, Q2)

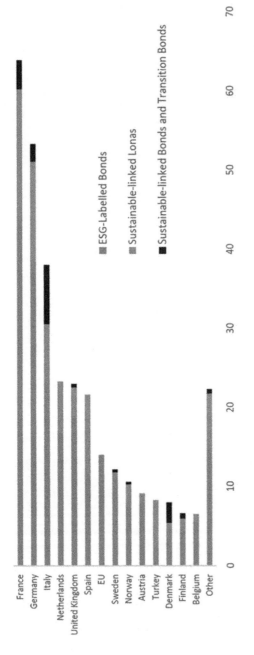

Source: The Association for Financial Markets in Europe (2023) *Sustainable Finance Report – Q2 2023.* https://www.afme.eu/Portals/0/DispatchFeaturedImages/AFME%20Sustainable%20Finance%20Report%20-%20Q2%202023—1.pdf (Accessed: 19.11.2023).

Figure 6.3   European ESG bond and loan issuance by country: EURbn (2023 YTD, Q2)

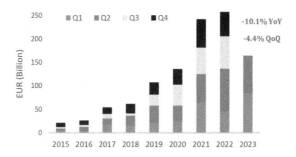

Source: The Association for Financial Markets in Europe (2023). *Sustainable Finance Report – Q2 2023*. https://www.afme.eu/Portals/0/DispatchFeaturedImages /AFME%20Sustainable%20Finance%20Report%20-%20Q2%202023—1.pdf (Accessed: 19.11.2023).

Figure 6.4   European green bond issuance

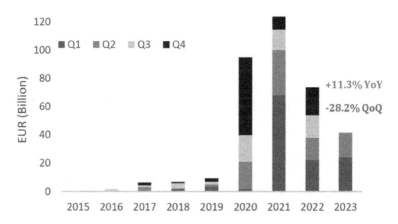

Source: The Association for Financial Markets in Europe (2023). *Sustainable Finance Report – Q2 2023*. https://www.afme.eu/Portals/0/DispatchFeaturedImages /AFME%20Sustainable%20Finance%20Report%20-%20Q2%202023—1.pdf (Accessed: 19.11.2023).

Figure 6.5   European social bond issuance

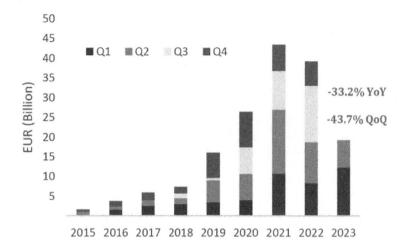

Source: The Association for Financial Markets in Europe (2023). *Sustainable Finance Report – Q2 2023*. https://www.afme.eu/Portals/0/DispatchFeaturedImages /AFME%20Sustainable%20Finance%20Report%20-%20Q2%202023—1.pdf (Accessed: 19.11.2023).

Figure 6.6   *European sustainable bond issuance*

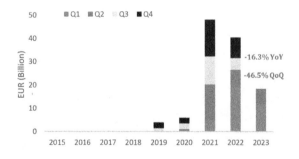

Source: The Association for Financial Markets in Europe (2023) *Sustainable Finance Report – Q2 2023*. https://www.afme.eu/Portals/0/DispatchFeaturedImages /AFME%20Sustainable%20Finance%20Report%20-%20Q2%202023—1.pdf (Accessed: 19.11.2023).

Figure 6.7   *European sustainable-linked and transition bond issuance*

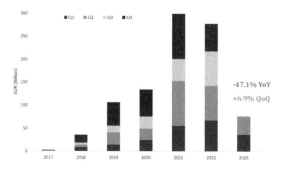

Source: The Association for Financial Markets in Europe (2023) *Sustainable Finance Report – Q2 2023*. https://www.afme.eu/Portals/0/DispatchFeaturedImages /AFME%20Sustainable%20Finance%20Report%20-%20Q2%202023—1.pdf (Accessed: 19.11.2023).

Figure 6.8   *European sustainability-linked and green-linked loan issuance (2017–2023, Q1)*

be higher than in 2022, because the YoY decline in H1 2023 amounted to nearly 50%.

The largest share in the European ESG Securitization issuance since 2016 has been held by residential mortgage-backed securitisations (RMBS) (Figure 6.9). Only in 2017 and 2020, when a large issue of on balance sheet asset-backed securities (ABS) took place, was the share of RMBS in the total issuance not the largest. In 2021, ESG Securitisation's total issuance reached a record EUR 8 billion. In 2022, the volume of issuance decreased several times. An increase in emissions can be expected in 2023, as after the first half of the year, its value approached the total value of emissions in 2022.

Looking at European ESG securitisation issuance by country, it can be noticed that the Netherlands is the only country that has issued ESG securitisations almost every year since 2016 (except for 2020) (Figure 6.10). However, the volume of issuance in the Netherlands, although stable, is not high (approximately EUR 0.5 billion). The remaining countries issued ESG securitisation only n specific years. For example, France in 2017, 2020, and 2021, with its share in total emissions in 2017 being the largest (over EUR 2.5 billion). The UK had the largest share in the record total emissions from 2021, followed by Italy and France. In H1 2023, Spain issued ESG securitisation for the first time.

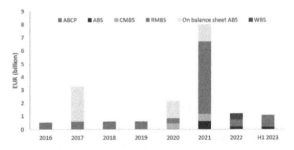

Notes: ABCP – asset-backed commercial paper; ABS – asset-backed securities; CMBS – commercial mortgage-backed securitisations; RMBS – residential mortgage-backed securitisations; WBS – whole business securitisation.

Source: The Association for Financial Markets in Europe (2023). *Sustainable Finance Report – Q2 2023*. https://www.afme.eu/Portals/0/DispatchFeaturedImages /AFME%20Sustainable%20Finance%20Report%20-%20Q2%202023—1.pdf (Accessed: 19.11.2023).

Figure 6.9   European ESG securitisation issuance by asset class

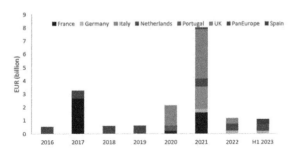

Source: The Association for Financial Markets in Europe (2023). *Sustainable Finance Report – Q2 2023*. https://www.afme.eu/Portals/0/DispatchFeaturedImages /AFME%20Sustainable%20Finance%20Report%20-%20Q2%202023—1.pdf (Accessed: 19.11.2023).

Figure 6.10   European ESG securitisation issuance by country

6.4   TOWARDS A CAPITAL MARKETS UNION

The initiative to create the Capital Market Union (CMU) was established in 2015 and its goal was to further integrate and develop capital markets in the European Union. Creating an integrated CMU would strengthen the economic structure of Europe and have a positive impact on the euro area (Panetta, 2023):

- It would make it easier to invest in the capital markets of the entire euro area and have that area benefit from it. The current barriers between capital markets in individual countries discourage investors from investing across borders. The creation of a CMU would contribute to increasing the flow of investments throughout the euro area, which would diversify risk and mitigate the effects of possible shocks.
- The CMU would complement the traditional channels of obtaining external funds (i.e., bank loans) to finance key innovations from the point of view of the concept of sustainable development, i.e., projects in the energy area (reduction of greenhouse gas emissions, departure from fossil fuels, and increasing the use of renewable energy sources) and technology. In 2019, UNCTAD estimated that to achieve the Sustainable Development Goals by 2030, total annual investment in sectors relevant to sustainable development would need to be between USD 3.3 trillion and USD 4.5 trillion, implying an annual financing gap of approximately USD 2.5 trillion (Doumbia and Lauridsen, 2019).
- CMU would increase the effectiveness of the monetary policy of the European Central Bank (ECB) by contributing to the timely, smooth, and even transmission of monetary policy to enterprises and households.
- Difficulties in creating an integrated CMU resulted mainly from different levels of capital market development in individual countries, which were particularly visible in many countries of Southern and Central and Eastern Europe (CEE), where capital markets are very limited.

In September 2020, a set of measures to revitalize the Capital Markets Union was proposed, covering four main areas: EU business financing, market infrastructure, retail investment, and the internal market. Legislative proposals in this regard are in the process of being adopted and concern the creation of a single access point (ESAP) for information on EU companies, the improvement of the legal framework for the European Long-Term Investment Fund (ELTIF), the Directive on Alternative Investment Fund Managers (AIFM); and the review of the Markets in Financial Instruments Regulation (MiFIR) regulation.

The next set of proposals were presented in December 2022 and focused on corporate insolvency and proposals to strengthen settlements in the EU. In June 2023, the Commission also proposed new rules to make withholding tax procedures in the EU more efficient and secure.

Since 2015, legislation has been adopted to develop EU securitisation markets and thus increase companies' access to finance, harmonise prudential rules for investment firms, and ease investment conditions for European venture capital in order to promote the financing of such capital. The regulations on public listing of EU companies, harmonisation of national bankruptcy systems, were also simplified, and problems related to the taxation of financial instruments were solved (Eurofi, 2023). However, the capital market remains fragmented.

REFERENCES

Association for Financial Markets in Europe. (2023). Sustainable Finance Report – Q2 2023. https://www.afme.eu/Portals/0/DispatchFeaturedImages /AFME%20Sustainable%20Finance%20Report%20-%20Q2%202023-1.pdf (Accessed: 19.11.2023).

Climate Bonds Initiative (2017). *The role of exchanges in accelerating the growth of the green bond market.* https://www.climatebonds.net/resources/ reports/role-exchanges-accelerating-growth-green-bond-market   (Accessed: 20.11.2023).

Doumbia D., & Lauridsen, M. L. (2019). *Closing the SDG Financing Gap— Trends and Data.* https://pdfs.semanticscholar.org/dbbf/e0cebd52906b7f7 eae4896d1a7806df6ec77.pdf (Accessed: 20.11.2023).

Eurofi. (2023). *Capital Markets Union.* https://www.eurofi.net/current-topics/ capital-markets-union/ (Accessed: 20.11.2023).

Konfederacja Lewiatan. (2021). *Zrównoważone finanse. Krótki przewodnik dla firm.* https://lewiatan.org/wp-content/uploads/2022/01/Zrownowazone -finanse-przewodnik-dla-firm.pdf (Accessed: 14.11.2023).

United Nations. (n.d.). Roadmap for Sustainable Capital Markets. https:// sdgs.un.org/partnerships/roadmap-sustainable-capital-markets (Accessed: 24.02.2024)

Panetta, F. (2023, August 30). Europe needs to think bigger to build its capital markets union. European Central Bank. https://www.ecb.europa .eu/press/blog/date/2023/html/ecb.blog230830~cfe3be0960.en.html (Accessed: 17.11.2023).

Pichola, I., Gasiński, T., & Średzińska, K. (2021). *Ratingi ESG – jaką dają wartość i jak się do nich dobrze przygotować?* Deloitte. https://www2 .deloitte.com/pl/pl/pages/zarzadzania-procesami-i-strategiczne/articles/esg -ratingi-jak-sie-przygotowac-jaka-daja-wartosc.html (Accessed: 20.11.2023).

Scheidig, F. (2023, May 9). *Capital markets can lead the way in transition finance.* OMFIF. https://www.omfif.org/2023/05/capital-markets-can-lead -the-way-in-transition-finance/ (Accessed: 18.11.2023).

Stoian, A. and Iorgulescu, F. (2019). Sustainable Capital Market. In M. Ziolo and B. Sergi (Eds.), *Financing Sustainable Development* (pp. 193–226). Palgrave Studies in Impact Finance. Cham: Palgrave Macmillan. https:// doi.org/10 .1007/978-3-030-16522-2_8.

United Nations. (n.d.). Roadmap for Sustainable Capital Markets. https:// sdgs.un.org/partnerships/roadmap-sustainable-capital-markets (Accessed: 24.02.2024)

United Nations Conference on Trade and Development. (2023). *World Investment Report 2023 Investing in sustainable energy for all*. United Nations. https:// unctad.org/system/files/official-document/wir2023_ch03_en.pdf (Accessed: 20.11.2023).

7. Challenges, prospects and recommendations of financial markets in the scope of SDGs

Beata Zofia Filipiak

7.1 INITIATIVES AND REGULATIONS DETERMINING CHANGES IN THE FINANCIAL MARKETS TOWARDS THE IMPLEMENTATION OF SDGs

Climate change is an important factor of instability in the financial market due to the risk of losses, the need to incur costs of hedging against risk, and the impact of non-financial factors. The basic act for building the regulatory environment for financial markets was the United Nations Environment Program Financial Initiative (UNEP FI). UNEP FI carries out its tasks through recommendations and guidelines in the field of banking, insurance, and investments (Kristić, 2013).

The European Union positively influences on financial markets towards the implementation of the SDGsthrough directives (such as obligatory regulations for members, with greater impact), good practices, sets of guidelines, or recommendations (they create optional rules for member countries) (UN, 2015). Institutions operating on the financial market are affected by climate change, and the impacting non-financial factors force them to make changes to business models or affect the profitability and profitability achieved. In order to be able to effectively influence changes, both obligatory and optional regulations are created regarding the legal environment conducive to creating changes towards sustainability. The most important mandatory regulations affecting financial markets include:

- BASEL II and BASEL III (operational risk standards, risk monitoring) are addressed to financial institutions, in particular banks, having a direct impact, regarding risk management, including environmental risk, and valuation of assets, including those expressed in environmental risk (Deloitte, 2023a);
- Directive 2014/95/EU of the European Parliament and of the Council of 22 October 2014 amending Directive 2013/34/EU as regards disclosure of non-financial and diversity information by certain large undertakings and groups (called the Non-financial Disclosure Reporting Directive – NFRD). Regulation relevant to financial institutions, in particular banks, and to enterprises and institutions (business), having an indirect impact, regarding imposing an obligation to disclose ESG factors in order to provide investors and other interested parties with a more complete picture of their development, performance, position and impact of their activities;
- Regulation (EU) 2016/1011 of the European Parliament and of the Council of 8 June 2016 on indices used as benchmarks in financial instruments and financial contracts or to measure the performance of investment funds and amending Directives 2008/48/EC and 2014/17/EU and Regulation (EU) No 596/2014. Regulation addressed to financial institutions, in particular investment funds, having an indirect impact, regarding the use of benchmarks;
- Commission Delegated Regulation (EU) 2017/2359 of 21 September 2017 supplementing Directive (EU) 2016/97 of the European Parliament and of the Council with regard to information requirements and conduct of business rules applicable to the distribution of insurance-based investment products. Regulation addressed to financial institutions, in particular financial intermediaries and insurance companies, having a direct impact, regarding ensuring harmonization of the regulatory framework for distribution standards of insurance investment products;
- Directive (EU) 2017/541 of the European Parliament and of the Council of 15 March 2017 on combating terrorism and replacing Council Framework Decision 2002/475/JHA and amending Council Decision 2005/671/JHA. Regulation addressed to financial institutions, in particular banks and listed companies, having an indirect impact, regarding ensuring the transparency of remuneration of persons managing and supervising listed companies;
- Regulation (EU) 2019/2088 of the European Parliament and of the Council of 27 November 2019 on sustainability-related disclosures

in the financial services sector. Regulation addressed to financial institutions, in particular banks, with a direct impact, regarding disclosures in financial statements of the impact of ESG factors on operational activities;

- Regulation (EU) 2019/2089 of the European Parliament and of the Council of 27 November 2019 amending Regulation (EU) 2016/1011 as regards EU Climate Transition Benchmarks, EU Paris-aligned Benchmarks and sustainability-related disclosures for benchmarks. Regulation addressed to financial institutions, in particular banks, with a direct impact, regarding the use of benchmarks;
- Regulation (EU) 2020/852 of the European Parliament and of the Council of 18 June 2020 on the establishment of a framework to facilitate sustainable investment, and amending Regulation (EU) 2019/2088;
- Directive (EU) 2022/2464 of the European Parliament and of the Council of 14 December 2022 amending Regulation (EU) No 537/2014, Directive 2004/109/EC, Directive 2006/43/EC and Directive 2013/34/EU, as regards corporate sustainability reporting. The regulation (Corporate Sustainability Reporting Directive, CSRD) introducing the obligation to report non-financially and uniform reporting standards by introducing one mandatory type of standard that applies to all entities, including financial institutions.

The Corporate Sustainability Reporting Directive (CSRD) amends the applicable NFRD directive. This directive lays the foundation for common, international regulations in the area of reporting and facilitates the possibility of monitoring support from the financial markets towards the implementation of the SDGs. Optional regulations are important for the development of financial markets towards building responsible and sustainable finance, supporting climate change while respecting ESG factors. They constitute both good practices and detail the regulatory environment. The most important include:

- ISO26000, which refers to the concept of socially responsible business, providing guidelines on the principles of social responsibility and stakeholder engagement. It covers key areas and issues related to social responsibility, applies to all financial institutions and business (market participants) and includes ways of integrating responsible behavior which is direct in nature;

- Equator Principles (EPs) – a risk management framework, adopted by financial institutions, for determining, assessing and managing environmental and social risk in projects, their task is to ensure socially and environmentally responsible financing through markets of large-scale infrastructure, mining and energy projects. They appliy to all financial institutions and businesses (market participants) and include ways of integrating responsible behavior which is direct in nature;
- United Nations Environment Program Finance Initiative – an agreement allowing the introduction of environmental issues into the current operation of financial institutions and puts emphasis on financing pro-environmental practices and technologies. Takingook the form of a UNEP FI statement, it applies to all financial institutions and businesses (market participants) and also includes ways of integrating responsible behavior which is direct in nature;
- GRI Standards, Sustainable Finance Disclosure Regulation (SFDR) and regulatory technical standards (RTS);
- European green bond standard– this plays an increasingly important role in financing assets needed for the low-carbon transition economy; it provides guidance for investors who want to invest in sustainable and climate-friendly projects; it harmonizes with the Taxonomy; and allows for the assessment that issuers have a tool to demonstrate, that they are funding legitimate green projects aligned with the EU Taxonomy and investors buying the bonds will be able to more easily assess, compare and trust that their investments are sustainable;
- EU Taxonomy for sustainable activities – a cornerstone of the EU's sustainable finance, it applies to all financial institutions and investors, is direct and obligatory in nature;
- A framework and an important financial market transparency tool, the task of the Taxonomy is to help direct investments to the economic activities most needed for the transition, in line with the European Green Deal objectives. It is a classification system that defines criteria for economic activities that are aligned with a net zero trajectory by 2050 and the SDGs; it applies to all financial institutions, entities and businesses (market participants); and it is direct and obligatory in nature.

It should be emphasized that the regulatory process is not over, as new challenges and needs related to the implementation of the SDGs are constantly emerging. However, it can be indicated that the activities undertaken so far have led to the development of basic principles that should be applied when financing the SDG goals through the financial market. Five basic principles should be distinguished (Borregaard, 2023):

- Clearly defining the goals, calibrating them in terms of Sustainability Performance Targets (SPTs) – this concerns the methods of using funds from the issue, the adequacy of the selection of the instrument, as well as calibrating the SPTs on KPIs;
- Establishing a framework for the evaluation and selection process of projects financed from financial instruments – the framework should be based on the principle of transparency and transparency of decisions, defining the rules of project eligibility, assessing the risk associated with project implementation, and taking into account non-financial risk (SDGs), including the presentation mode in the decision-making processes data regarding the applied sustainability and SDG principles in the context of the issuer's overarching activities, its goals and its development strategy in connection with the implemented SDGs;
- Fund management – based on the use of separate sub-accounts and monitoring the use of collected funds for purposes related to the implementation of SDGs, introducing transparency of reporting in this area;
- Reporting and verification – the market participant should provide information on the use of funds from instruments obtained on the market, should be prepared to enable verification by an independent auditor, as well as with such detail that the achievement of each SPT goal for each KPI can be assessed.
- Build good practice and share your experience.

The indicated solutions constitute an important point of reference to standards created and implemented only on European financial markets (GISA, 2021). Solutions for changes in financial markets towards the implementation of the SDGs indicate the multiplicity of standards and the lack of uniformity of the provisions they contain. On the one hand, the indicated barrier slows down the development of financial markets oriented towards achieving the SDGs, but on the other hand, change leaders, in particular the EU, create important solutions, standards and good practices that have cognitive and application value among international organizations or individual countries.

7.2 EVALUATION OF CHANGES IN THE OFFER AND USE OF SUSTAINABLE FINANCIAL MARKET INSTRUMENTS

Climate change and the emerging legal and regulatory environment affect everyone without exception. The largest financial institutions in the world have no doubt that only joint and decisive actions can ensure the survival of our civilization, and the introduction of rigorous regulations, supported by good practices, can bring results. Sustainable finance, taking into account social and environmental needs with the support of corporate social responsibility, is today the basic foundation for the activities of financial market leaders in the world, especially in Europe. Financial institutions most often support six environmental goals: climate change mitigation, climate change adaptation, sustainable use of water and marine resources, transition to a circular economy, pollution prevention, biodiversity protection, and the ecosystem.

With a financial markets focus, it is necessary to point out five key trends creating changes in the offer and use of sustainable financial market instruments (Fig. 7.1.).

For the development of financial markets and their offers towards the implementation of the SDG goals, two legal regulations are of fundamental importance in EU countries: Regulation (EU) 2020/852 and Directive (EU) 2022/2464 (implementation of CSRD). They are the ones that create changes in the offer and directions in the use of sustainable financial market instruments.

On March 10, 2021, the provisions of Regulation (EU) 2019/2088 of the European Parliament and of the Council, abbreviated as SFDR, came into force in EU countries. The SFDR imposed a number of obligations on financial market participants (including insurance companies providing insurance investment products and investment companies providing portfolio management services) and financial advisors related to the disclosure of information related to sustainable development. These obligations are divided into disclosures made at the entity and product levels. Entity disclosures oblige entities to maintain transparency in the scope of their activities by, for example, publishing on their websites strategies regarding the introduction of sustainable development risks into their activities (i.e. the impact of ESG factors on the value of investments). Product disclosures require obligated entities to, among other things, provide clients with a description of how sustainable development risks are introduced in investment decisions made or services provided before concluding a contract (SFDR, 2020). The minimum scope of disclosure therefore concerns the provision of (SFDR, 2023; Barry et. al., 2023):

Information on the adopted strategy regarding sustainable development risk when making investment decisions (SR, Sustainability Risks), includes:

• description of the method for determining the list of risks and prioritizing the main adverse effects on sustainable development and indicators;
• description of the main adverse impacts on sustainable development and a description of any actions taken to address them;
• information on compliance with codes of responsible business conduct and internationally recognized due diligence and reporting standards;
• information on disclosures regarding the negative impact of investment decisions on sustainable development factors (ASIs, adverse sustainability impacts);
• information on the remuneration policy, including information on how to ensure consistency of these policies with the introduction of sustainable development risks into the business.

In addition to disclosures, additional obligations have also been introduced that should be met before concluding a contract by entities from the financial services sector. These include (van Eenennaam et al., 2023):

• The obligation to explain to the client how sustainability risks are introduced in the investment decisions made by financial entities and the results of the assessment of the likely impact of Sustainability Risks (SRs) on the return of the financial products that are made available.
• Entities providing information about ASIs (adverse sustainability impacts) on their websites will be obliged to take them into account at the stage of concluding the contract.

The establishment of the taxonomy by regulation of the European Parliament and of the Council of 18 June 2020 is the first step in the implementation of the Action Plan on financing sustainable economic growth. The concept of taxonomy in the context of sustainable development should be understood as a set of criteria, the fulfillment of which means that a given activity can be considered environmentally sustainable. Taxonomy is a concept used colloquially, but legally the taxonomy functions as a "framework facilitating sustainable investments" (Regulation EU 2020/852, pp. 13–43). Business activities are assessed according to the criteria specified in the taxonomy. This activity is marked using the European NACE classification system. On this basis, it is possible to determine the extent to which the entire activity of a specific company or other type of entity is sustainable, and then only on this basis is it possible to assess the degree of environmental sustainability of a financial product or investment portfolio. The taxonomy applies to investors, financial intermediaries, and entrepreneurs. The former will have to review their portfolios and investment selection strategies. Financial institutions, in turn, will have to declare the extent to which the products they offer comply with the taxonomy. Financial products should be understood as open-end investment funds, insurance investment products, pension funds, individual portfolio management, and insurance and investment consulting. However, clients of financial institutions will be obliged to report what percentage of their turnover, capital expenditure (CapEx), and operational expenditure (OpEx) corresponds to sustainable activities within the meaning of the taxonomy. Infrastructure projects that do not meet the principles of sustainable development within the meaning of the taxonomy will have difficulty obtaining financing (UE, 2021).

Both the SFDR and the Taxonomy Regulation required the development of European supervisory authorities (i.e. the European Banking Authority [EBA], the European Securities and Markets Authority [ESMA], and the European Insurance and Occupational Pensions Authority [EIOPA]) acting through a common committee toward a series of regulatory technical standards ("RTSs"). Due to the late publication of the draft RTSs, the obligation to report in the scope specified therein was postponed from 2022 to the beginning of 2023. The RTS contains non-binding interpretative guidelines for obligated entities, but on the other hand, it may be the basis for a more stringent approach by supervisors during the transitional period (Barry et. al., 2023).

Transparency serves to create trust among societies, organizations, and their stakeholders, including investors. It is not only about the planet but also about relationships within society, between people, and between corporations, enterprises, and governments. That is why companies, entities, and other organizations focus on disclosing the information. The GRI Standards and SASB Standards provide compatible standards for such disclosures. These two standards are mutually supportive and designed to fulfill different purposes. The conception of sustainability reporting has widened and now it envisages economic, environmental, and social elements reporting for measuring corporate financial performance (Abeyratne & Morais, 2021). The GRI reporting framework guides organizations to select topics that reflect their most significant economic, environmental, and social impacts in consultation with their stakeholders (GRI and SASB Report, 2021). The GRI Standards strengthen the very foundations of all reporting, delivering the highest level of transparency for organizational impacts on the economy, environment, and society. The GRI is used to respond to emerging regulatory disclosure needs, such as the EU Corporate Sustainability Reporting Directive (CSRD) and the IFRS plans for enterprise value standards (GRI, 2023). The GRI Standards 2021 introduce a broader approach to reporting. This is expressed in: (1) a broader form of reporting on due diligence and human rights issues than before, (2) a change in the approach to basic issues and main reporting principles, and (3) a focus on a precise and detailed definition of the materiality analysis process. The GRI Standards 2021 maintain the existing thematic standards, i.e., in the economic (GRI 201 and subsequent), environmental (301 and subsequent), and social (401 and subsequent) areas (Filipiak and Dylewski, 2020).

SASB's industry-specific standards identify the sustainability-related risks and opportunities most likely to affect a company's financial condition (i.e. its balance sheet), operating performance (i.e. its income statement), risk profile (i.e. cost of capital), or long-term enterprise value (SASB, 2023). All of these factors impact the company's current and future market valuation. These elements are important from the point of view of the functioning of potential issuers of financial instruments related to the implementation of sustainable development goals on financial markets. The SASB Standards identify sustainability topics for the typical company in an industry. SASB's process requires evidence of investor interest and evidence of financial impact for a topic to be included in the Standards (KPMG, 2023). These standards include disclosure topics across five sustainability dimensions, including environmental, human and social capital, business model and innovation, and leadership and governance (GRI and SASB Report, 2021).

From August 2022, the International Sustainable Standards Board (ISSB) of the IFRS Foundation took over responsibility for the SASB Standards, which will contribute not only to the strengthening and development of SASB Standards but to their wider promotion as an important instrument for building transparency in the implementation of the SDGs and as an instrument playing role in monitoring the implementation of the SDGs.

With regard to work on regulating greenwashing, the point is to develop a mutual position on defining the concept; the European Commission is expected to formulate a directive to regulate "green claims" made by organizations. As indicated in practice, the risk of greenwashing may result from inaction rather than greenwashing alone (Michaelsen & Ray, 2023).

From the perspective of implementing the SDGs, it is important to know the current structure of financing the transformation and the origin of the sources of capital. This clarity can undoubtedly be ensured by financial markets by implementing taxonomies and allowing sustainable investment products to be traded. Maintaining the trend of financing climate change in the global economy towards a low-carbon reality and increasing the role and position of "transition bonds" in the offer of financial markets are also vital (Shrimali, 2021). Development of "sustainability-linked" structures, supported both by the International Capital Market Association (ICMA) and the Loan Market Association (LMA), is another aspect (Michaelsen & Ray, 2023).

Still the most important factor in the total redirection of the financial markets towards sustainability is the rise of the green bond market (and sustainable finance products more broadly). Further actions would be to implement and disseminate the ICMA Green Bond Principles and a strong reactivation of the so-called "transition label." It is expected that the concept of "hybrid" structures may also soon enter the conversation within sustainable finance as market participants look to new and different ways to stay relevant to stakeholders. The novel structure combines a "use-of-proceeds" approach on the framework level with a "sustainability-linked" one on the asset level (Michaelsen & Ray, 2023). Concessional climate financing for individual countries is being introduced, and structuring blended financing packages for investments is also planned (World Bank, 2023).

To sum up, changes in the offer and use of sustainable financial market instruments will require, on the one hand, reducing ESG risk by managing and transferring risk, providing sustainable services and offering sustainable financial products, but also transferring knowledge and good practices, introducing financial innovations towards enabling financing the implementation of the SDGs and the implementation of ESG solutions (especially reporting).

7.3   THE IMPACT OF ESG FACTORS ON THE FINANCIAL MARKET IN THE CONTEXT OF CLIMATE CHANGE

Currently, the business landscape is shaped by issues related to climate change, the loss of natural areas, the recurring demand for racial equality and improved working conditions, the COVID-19 pandemic, and changing requirements for the role of corporations. A new business resilience is being created, which forces entities to justify their market existence through greater involvement in creating sustainable value that covers the broadly understood needs of people and our planet. This action also applies to financial markets, which, together with other financial institutions, participate in the transformation of their clients towards sustainability, and through the use of taxonomies show how the SDGs are implemented.

Taking into account the far-reaching implementation of climate solutions and, above all, the threats posed by climate change, pollution, and degradation of the natural environment, it should be stated that ESG factors concern issues that are currently of great importance to the entire world.

This means that there is no turning back from implementing ESG solutions on a global scale. We can therefore point to the key impact of ESG factors on the financial market in the context of climate change. Financial markets, as well as cooperating entities and clients able to implement the principles of ESG information disclosure, are on the way to skillfully incorporating ESG factors into their strategic plans, thus better preparing for risk management, including environmental and social ones, while obtaining guarantees for stakeholders to maintain lasting value and increase resilience in a world driven by new rules. In Figure 7.2 the most important factors influencing the impact of ESG factors on financial markets are indicated.

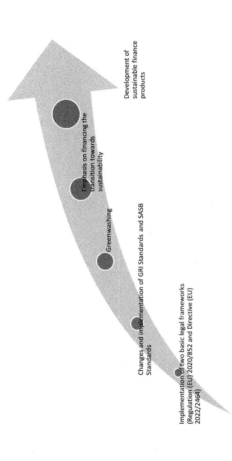

Source: Own elaboration.

Figure 7.1   Key trends creating changes in the offer and use of sustainable instruments

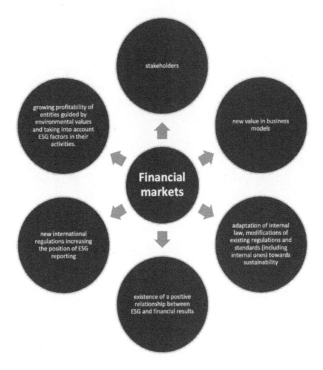

Source: Own elaboration.

Figure 7.2   *The most important factors influencing the impact of*
                 ESG factors on financial markets

Market entities, under the influence of ESG factors, design products and services aimed at "consumers" who have more and more knowledge about the importance of ecology and corporate social responsibility. Consumers consciously choose products and services, guided not only by price or usability, but above all by ESG criteria (Boufounou et al., 2023). Society, including employees, suppliers, business partners, community members, and activists, in the general sense of the word, have become equal participants/stakeholders – direct dialogue on expectations towards various companies in terms of achieving SDGs and taking into account ESG factors in businesses and activities. Stakeholders value transparency because it allows them to make informed choices. Increasing pressure to meet SDG targets and incorporate ESG factors may result in a company's ability to meet key environmental and social expectations impacting public support for their operations. Greater transparency regarding ESG factors can help attract new customers; increase interest among potential employees and then retain them; reduce costs and increase the effectiveness of activities; and reduce the risk and potential loss of good reputation. Thus, it resutls in a better evaluation of and by the financial markets.

Meeting the requirements set by the sustainable market and creating new value towards sustainability is often associated with existing social expectations and the dynamics of development of the sustainable financial market (Ziolo et al., 2022). This factor may encourage entities to rebuild their business models and create new value. As companies begin to analyze their business through the prism of ESG, they must clearly define the key business value drivers and make an effort to measure and identify those elements that currently matter. Thus, new value is created (focused on ESG and the implementation of SDGs) in their business models (Scott & Pankratz, 2021).

New business models are accepted by potential investors on financial markets if they explain how the decisions they make reflect the interests of their stakeholders and the environment and the strategy is related to the implementation of the SDGs in the context of being in line with the idea of sustainable development. What type of financial assembly is used (sustainable financial products) also becomes important. The adoption of environmental obligations by financial markets and their clients shows stakeholders that decisions are made in accordance with the idea of ESG, which builds trust, and trust is the basis of business value (Ziolo et al., 2023).

Investor decisions allow us to see that there is a positive relationship between taking into account ESG risk in decisions and the achieved and positive effects of operations. The analysis shows that investors see potential opportunities in companies that take into account ESG risk, which is associated with involvement in climate issues and taking actual actions to implement the SDGs. Hence, such entities have and will have easier access to investment capital (Stiadi, 2023).

Though ESG investing may have social benefits (Cornell, 2021), it ought to be emphasized that for ESG to bring real profits, it is necessary to make the right choice of company and the use of investment opportunities requires obtaining high-quality, comparable data. Hence, there is a demand to define global standards of sustainable development and to introduce more restrictive ESG reporting, which affects the importance of the taxonomy (Ibisz & Osowiecka, 2023).

The limited availability of comparable data makes it difficult for investors to evaluate companies' activities, and according to activists, it creates room for abuse (e.g. greenwashing). Therefore, work is underway on common regulations in individual countries (not only in the EU, but also in the USA, among the G7 signatories (IOSCO 2021; UE, 2021). Common GRI standards are being introduced (as indicated). Common legal solutions, as well as their implementation, may contribute not only to a greater impact of non-financial factors on the implementation of SDG goals through disclosure but will also allow for a broader analysis of the phenomenon itself through access to consistent data.

7.4 RECOMMENDATIONS AND LIMITATIONS RELATED TO THE IMPLEMENTATION OF THE SDGS ON THE SUSTAINABLE FINANCIAL MARKET

CSR, which enables companies and the financial market to undertake certain small social commitments in freely selected areas, is important primarily from the point of view of companies. This means that CSR is not enough, and it is necessary to think holistically in the context of ESG, especially activities aimed at disclosing and minimizing ESG risk. This challenge has become real not only for financial markets but for stakeholders and companies that raise capital through the financial market. The basis for the changes is the cooperation of three partners: governments (local governments), financial institutions (financial markets), and business (Berrone et al., 2023). Based on recommendations and directional changes in the role of non-financial factors towards sustainability, the following recommendations were formulated.

One challenge will be for government and local governments to figure out where it makes sense for them to lead on climate change, what types of changes to support and where they might make a bigger impact in a supporting role to the private sector. Currently, many governments talk a lot and point to the need for help, but their actions are ineffective.

In order to effectively implement the SDGs, it is necessary to have an integrated financial model based on the public and market financial systems, and in particular financial institutions such as banks, stock exchanges, and active financial intermediaries. Financial institutions which are interdependent and related in terms of meeting the criteria of sustainable financing should support the implementation of common standards, especially the assessment of the implementation of SDGs and the implementation of ESG. What does the green light mean for the implementation of common reporting solutions?

- An efficient and effective system for collecting and flowing information on the implementation of SDGs and disclosures.
- The inability of the public financial system to keep up (and not overtake) comprehensive solutions in the field of ESG should be supported by good practices from financial institutions for the public financial system for financing environmental goals through legal regulations.
- The integration of financial policy and sustainable development policy is a goal for many governments, especially EU countries, but it is necessary to develop common monitoring indicators and common goals to ensure integration of the financial sphere and reality.
- The information policy (effects and consequences) for the implementation of the SDGs should be expanded based on the existing reporting system divided into main market actors (financial institutions, banks, enterprises, and the public sphere). This will allow monitoring both support from financial institutions for the implementation of SDGs and ESG implementation, but also the achievements of enterprises and governments in creating climate change towards sustainability.
- Further work is necessary to monitor the development of GRI standards, taxonomies, and their efficient implementation, as well as developing a system for exchanging good practices in this area.

The new reporting will be subject to mandatory audit by designated certification units and placing the report in the official report database. Failure to comply with the obligation will result in financial penalties. To facilitate the uniform preparation of reports by companies, the European Financial Reporting Council, i.e. European Sustainability Reporting Standards (ESRS), is working on uniform standards. The implementation of taxonomies and standardization is undoubtedly limited by the standards themselves. Today, it is known that entities must also include information in the reports from the following areas: energy transformation, the circular economy, biodiversity protection, the demand for water, pollutants, i.e. emissions of gases and dust into the air, and social and employee issues. The lack of uniform patterns, delays in their implementation, lack of international consent, or negative lobbying and business interests may affect and delay joint actions to implement uniform solutions. Delaying actions will affect the efficiency of markets towards sustainability and will even delay the effects of transformation. There will be negative effects of greenwashing, which will negatively impact potential stakeholders as well as sustainable shareholders of financial markets.

Important to achieving the SDGs is the Science Based Targets initiative (SBTi) that has developed a net zero standard for enterprises so that it is consistent with the Sustainable Development Goals (Net-Zero, 2023). To implement the developed standard, there are at least four limitations. First, there is no consistency of opinion on the extent of climate impacts regarding the types of greenhouse gases. Some companies refer to all greenhouse gases (GHGs), others only selectively to CO^2 (Net-Zero, 2023). There is also a lack of consistency as to the scope of enterprise operations to which the net zero target applies. Thirdly, there are significant differences in the implemented strategy to combat climate change. The fourth problem is the scope of the SDGs (2050), and the transitional goals (so-called milestones) are not specified. For the achievement of the SDGs and the implementation of ESG, these four issues constitute a serious limitation (Net-Zero, 2023).

Many financial institutions understand the need to finance climate change along with the opportunities that the transformation brings, as well as the risks associated with it. Thanks to their support, efforts are being made to engage market participants and incorporate ESG factors into mainstream financial practices. Financial institutions operating in financial markets are becoming a catalyst in disclosing ESG information, promoting reporting or even requiring it (over 80%). The leading role of these institutions in achieving green goals gives companies a unique opportunity to engage and develop effective transformation paths based on the standards of financial institutions, as well as based on benchmarks of other financial market participants.

REFERENCES

Abeyratne, D., & Morais, N. (2021). Sustainable reporting: An analysis of disclosure practices of selected business organizations in Sri Lanka. *Sri Lanka Journal of Management Studies*, 3(1), 127. doi:https://doi. org/10.4038/sljms.v3i1.68

Barry, D., Collington, D., Adcock, M., Johnson, M. (2023). The European Commission's review of SFDR. Radical suggestions, uncertain outcomes

https://kpmg.com/xx/en/home/insights/2023/09/the-european-commissions
-review-of-sfdr.html

Berrone, P., Rousseau, H.E., Ricart, J.E., Brito, E. & Giuliodori, A. (2023). How
can research contribute to the implementation of sustainable development
goals? An interpretive review of SDG literature in management. *International
Journal of Management Reviews*, 25, 318–339.https://doi.org/10.1111/ijmr
.12331

Borregaard. (2023) Green Financing Framework. Borregaard, June 2023 https://
ml-eu.globenewswire.com/Resource/Download/504295a4-28f0-42e6-b46b
-b7e390d159c7

Boufounou, P., Moustairas, I., Toudas, K. & Melesios, Ch. (2023). ESGs and
Customer Choice: Some Empirical Evidence. *Circ. Econ. Sust.*, vol. 3, pp.
1841–1874 https://doi.org/10.1007/s43615-023-00251-8

Commission Delegated Regulation (EU) 2017/2359 of 21 September 2017
supplementing Directive (EU) 2016/97 of the European Parliament and of
the Council with regard to information requirements and conduct of business
rules applicable to the distribution of insurance-based investment products,
Document 32017R2359

Cornell, B. (2021) ESG preferences, risk and return. *European Financial
Management*, 27, (1), 12–19, DOI: 10.1111/eufm.12295

Deloitte. (2023a). US Basel III Endgame: Key changes, impacts and where to
Begin, 2023, Deloitte Development LLC

Deloitte. (2023b). Many financial services companies mobilize for ESG
reporting. https://www2.deloitte.com/us/en/pages/audit/articles/esg-survey/
financial-services-companies-sustainability-reporting.html

Directive (EU) 2017/541 of the European Parliament and of the Council of
15 March 2017 on combating terrorism and replacing Council Framework
Decision 2002/475/JHA and amending Council Decision 2005/671/JHA,
Document 32017L0541

Directive (EU) 2022/2464 of the European Parliament and of the Council of 14
December 2022 amending Regulation (EU) No 537/2014, Directive 2004/109/
EC, Directive 2006/43/EC and Directive 2013/34/EU, as regards corporate
sustainability reporting (Text with EEA relevance), Document 32022L2464

Directive 2014/95/EU of the European Parliament and of the Council of 22
October 2014 amending Directive 2013/34/EU as regards disclosure of non-
financial and diversity information by certain large undertakings and groups,
Document 32014L0095

European Commission, "Proposal for a directive of the European parliament
and of the council as regards corporate sustainability reporting," April 21,
2021

Filipiak, B.Z. and Dylewski, M. (2020). Sustainable financial reporting in
the context of ensuring sustainability of financial systems, in *Finance and
Sustainable Development*, ed. M. Ziolo, London: Routledge, 235–267

GISA. (2021). Global Sustainable Investment Review. Report 2020. The Global
Sustainable Investment Alliance (GSIA) 2021. http://www.gsi-alliance.org/
wp-content/uploads/2021/08/GSIR-20201.pdf

GRI and SASB. (2021). A Practical Guide to Sustainability Reporting Using GRI and SASB Standards, GRI AND SASB, with support from PWC, The Impact Management Project, and Climateworks Foundation, London 2021, https://www.globalreporting.org/media/mlkjpn1i/gri-sasb-joint-publication-april-2021.pdf

GRI. (2023). How to use the GRI Standards , https://www.globalreporting.org

Ibisz, M. & Osowiecka, M. (2023). Wstrząśnięte zostały fundamenty, czyli jak standardy ESG wpływają na biznes, rynki i regulacje. Trendy w raportowaniu zrównoważonego rozwoju i ujawnieńk limatycznych https://www2.deloitte.com/pl/pl/pages/zarzadzania-procesami-i-strategiczne/articles/wstrzasniete-zostaly-fundamenty-czyli-jak-standardy-ESG-wplywaja-na-biznes-rynki-i-regulacje.html

IOSCO. (2021). Report on sustainability-related issuer disclosures, June 2021. https://www.iosco.org/library/pubdocs/pdf/IOSCOPD678.pdf

KPMG. (2023). https://kpmg.com/pl/pl/blogs/home/posts/2023/01/standardy-gri-jakie-zmiany-obowiazuja-od-stycznia-2023-esg-blog.html

Michaelsen J. & Ray D. (2023). What to expect from the sustainable finance market in 2023, Nordea, https://www.nordea.com/en/news/what-to-expect-from-the-sustainable-finance-market-in-2023

Net-Zero. (2023). SBTi Corporate Net-Zero Standard, https://sciencebasedtargets.org/resources/files/Net-Zero-Standard.pdf.

Regulation (EU) 2016/1011 of thve European Parliament and of the Council of 8 June 2016 on indices used as benchmarks in financial instruments and financial contracts or to measure the performance of investment funds and amending Directives 2008/48/EC and 2014/17/EU and Regulation (EU) No 596/2014, Document 32016R101

Regulation (EU) 2019/2088 of the European Parliament and of the Council of 27 November 2019

Regulation (EU) 2019/2088 of the European Parliament and of the Council of 27 November 2019 on sustainability-related disclosures in the financial services sector, Document 32019R2088

Regulation (EU) 2019/2089 of the European Parliament and of the Council of 27 November 2019 amending Regulation (EU) 2016/1011 as regards EU Climate Transition Benchmarks, EU Paris-aligned Benchmarks and sustainability-related disclosures for benchmarks (Text with EEA relevance), Document 32019R2089

Regulation (EU) 2020/852 of the European Parliament and of the Council of 18 June 2020 on the establishment of a framework to facilitate sustainable investment, and amending Regulation (EU) 2019/2088), Document 32020R0852

SASB. (2023). SASB Standard Overview, The IFRS Foundation, 2023 https://sasb.org/standards/

Scott C. & Pankratz, D.K. (2021). Leading in a low-carbon future: A "system of systems" approach to addressing climate change, Deloitte Insights, May 24, https://www2.deloitte.com/us/en/insights/topics/strategy/low-carbon-future.html

SFDR. (2020). Sustainable Finance Disclosure Regulation (SFDR), PwC, Switzerland, https://www.pwc.ch/en/publications/2020/sustainable-finance-disclosure-regulation.pdf

SFDR. (2023). https://www.eurosif.org/policies/sfdr/

Stiadi, D. (2023). Moderating Environmental, Social, and Governance (ESG) risk in the relationship between investment decisions and firm value, IOP Conf. Ser., *Earth Environ. Sci.,* 1177, 012007, doi:10.1088/1755-1315/1177/1/012007

UE. (2021). EU comments from December 2021 on Article 8 of EU Taxonomy Regulation, https://finance.ec.europa.eu/system/files/2022-01/sustainable-finance-taxonomy-article-8-report-eligible-activities-assets-faq_en.pdf

UN. (2015). United Nations. 2015. Transforming our world: the 2030 Agenda for Sustainable Development. Resolution adopted by the General Assembly on 25 September 2015, A/RES/70/1

van Eenennaam, M. Huige – van de Loo, E. & Ali, K. (2023). SFDR compliance: A look into current status, challenges, and possible solutions, Deloitte, https://www2.deloitte.com/nl/nl/pages/financial-services/articles/sfdr-compliance.htmlWorld Bank. (2023). A New Era of Development. World Bank Annual Report, Washington, DC, 2023, https://openknowledge.worldbank.org/bitstreams/69332452-bfbb-4b09-bd60-f4932a43c89a/download

Ziolo M., Bak I., Cheba K., Filipiak B.Z., & Spoz A. (2023). Environmental, social, governance risk *versus* cooperation models between financial institutions and businesses. Sectoral approach and ESG risk analysis. *Front. Environ. Sci.,* Sec. Environmental Economics and Management, 10, https://doi.org/10.3389/fenvs.2022.1077947

Index